Movie Stars

RAY BONDS

CHARTWELL
BOOKS, INC.

This edition published by

CHARTWELL BOOKS, INC.
A Division of
BOOK SALES, INC.
114 Northfield Avenue
Edison, New Jersey 08837

ISBN 0-7858-2154-6
ISBN 978-0-785821-54-7

© 2006 by Compendium Publishing Ltd., 43 Frith Street, London
W1D 4SA, United Kingdom

Cataloging-in-Publication data is available from the Library of Congress

Designer Ian Hughes

Printed in China by Constant Printing Limited.

Acknowledgments
All images were supplied by EMPICS in the UK. EMPICS are also the
suppliers of Associated Press images to UK picture buyers and these have
been syndicated via EMPICS for this title (and are so credited at the end
of each relevant caption). For more information see www.empics.com.

INTRODUCTION

Presented in this book are a couple of hundred of the greatest movie stars ever to grace the big screen, from the "silents" to the present day. They include some actors who couldn't act that well but who nevertheless had such riveting screen presence that they became unquestionably great movie stars. They include stars who have played in comedies, musicals, wide-

John Wayne

Legendary macho movie star John Wayne, shown during the filming of "The Horse Soldiers," would probably turn in his grave if he saw the gay cowboys romancing in "Brokeback Mountain." (AP Photo via EMPICS)

sweeping historical epics, tense courtroom dramas, noisy war films, fabulous Westerns, stirring romances, seedy sex escapades, chilling horrors, scenically beautiful spectaculars, tales of courage and fortitude, true stories and works of mind-boggling fiction, costume dramas, episodes of extreme tenderness and terrifying violence, movies with a message and those that have generated heartwarming joy.

Some of the stars have performed in many of these categories, while others have become famous for being typecast (but good) in a single genre. Some movie stars have made it based merely on their good looks, the timbre of their speaking voice, or the way they move. Others have impressed by their dramatic performances or the sensitivity of their role-playing. Some have played themselves in every role they have undertaken, while yet others have adopted the finest intricacies of a wide range of various personalities.

Most of the stars have been entertaining, else they wouldn't be featured in this book. There have been literally thousands of movie stars, including those who have played the leading parts, and others who have stolen scenes as supporting acts. Many have received critical acclaim and have been honored with awards, and others who should have won but did not. Therefore the choice of who to include and who to leave out could only ever have been subjective: one cinemagoer's opinion will differ widely from that of another. One might consider Chaplin or Laurel & Hardy as sheer comic geniuses, while another might regard them as silly. One might consider Brando's "method" style as wooden, while another would marvel at his screen presence.

Whatever your opinion, the stars are presented in our A-Z section for your entertainment and enjoyment.

Jake Gyllenhaal

Jake Gyllenhaal, nominated for outstanding performance by a male actor in a supporting role for his work in "Brokeback Mountain," arrives for the 12th Annual Screen Actors Guild Awards, January 29, 2006, in Los Angeles. The movie world may well be lauding the filmmakers for their courage for portraying homosexuality in this "new Western," but will the general viewing public give it their approval? (AP Photo via EMPICS)

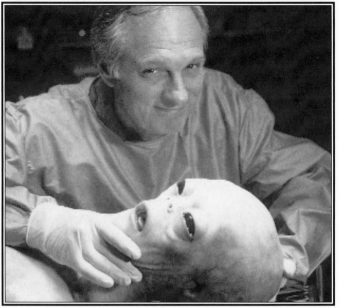

Ben Affleck

Ben Affleck poses at the Regent Beverly Wilshire Hotel in Los Angeles, December 6, 2003, before the premier of the sci-fi thriller "Paycheck" in which he stars. Affleck won an Oscar (with Matt Damon) for screenwriting the 1997 movie "Good Will Hunting." (AP Photo via EMPICS)

Alan Alda

In 2004 Alan Alda was nominated for an Academy Award for Best Supporting Actor for his role as Senator Ralph Owen Brewster in Martin Scorsese's film "The Aviator," although he is best known for his starring, writing, and directing roles in the TV series "M*A*S*H." Here he poses with a dummy during a break in taping the PBS series "Scientific American Frontiers," which Alda has hosted since 1993.

Woody Allen

Writer, director, and actor Woody Allen poses during the presentation to the press of his new film "Match Point" in Rome, December 21, 2005. Born in and influenced by New York City, Allen nevertheless has enjoyed tremendous support from fans in Europe, where it is rumored he will be shooting more movies form 2007 onward. (AP Photo via EMPICS)

Dana Andrews

A film clip from the 1948 movie "The Iron Curtain" shows Dana Andrews (second row back), performing in the Twentieth Century Fox production based on the personal story of Igor Gouzenko, former code clerk of the Russian Embassy in Ottawa, Canada. Andrews acted in many tense and sometimes romantic roles, and gave perhaps his best performance in the Oscar-winning "The Best Years Of Our Lives" in 1946. Born in 1909, he died in 1992. (AP Photo via EMPICS)

Julie Andrews

British actress and singer Dame Julie Andrews smiles during the presentation of her new romantic comedy, "The Princess Diaries 2: Royal Engagement," in Munich, Germany, September 23, 2004. The talented Academy Award-winning Andrews is best known for her musical movies "Mary Poppins" (1964) and "The Sound of Music" (1965).

Fred Astaire

Elegance personified, Fred Astaire (born 1899, died 1987) glided and tapped seemingly effortlessly across the silver screen in more than forty films (ten of them with Ginger Rogers), as well as performing well in a few dramatic roles, such as in "Towering Inferno" (1974), for which he received an Academy Award nomination for Best Supporting Actor. Here, he and Eleanor Powell dance to Cole Porter's "Begin the Beguine" in "Broadway Melody of 1940." (AP Photo via EMPICS)

Dan Aykroyd

A clip from the 1984 movie "Ghostbusters" shows Canadian comedian, actor, screenwriter, and musician Dan Aykroyd (center) with Bill Murray (left) and Harold Ramis. Aykroyd received an Academy Award nomination as Best Supporting Actor for his role in "Driving Miss Daisy" (1989). (AP Photo via EMPICS)

Lauren Bacall

Seen here in 1957 with Frank Sinatra, of whom she has been quoted as saying, "He wanted to be in the sack with everybody," the enduring Lauren Bacall got her big break into movie fame acting with Humphrey Bogart in the 1944 "To Have And Have Not." She was married to Bogart in 1945 until he died in 1957, and played opposite him in "The Big Sleep" (1946), "Dark Passage" (1947), and "Key Largo" (1948). In 1997 she received an Academy Award nomination as Best Actress in a Supporting Role in "The Mirror Has Two Faces."

Antonio Banderas

Famous for playing the title role in the action-packed movies "The Mask Of Zorro" (1998) and "The Legend of Zorro" (2005) opposite Catherine Zeta-Jones, Spanish actor Antonio Banderas also put in a creditable performance as the narrator Che in "Evita" (1996), starring Madonna. He married actress Melanie Griffith in 1996.

Brigitte Bardot

French actress Brigitte Bardot poses with a huge sombrero she brought back from Mexico as she arrives at Orly Airport in Paris, France, May 27, 1965. Bardot was in Mexico working on the production of the motion picture "Viva Maria." It was her seventeenth film, the 1956 "And God Created Woman," that launched her into international sex-kitten superstardom. Bardot retired in 1974, having appeared in more than fifty movies, and launched herself into animal rights and other controversial issues. (AP Photo via EMPICS)

Drew Barrymore

Born in 1975 in California with acting in her blood—granddaughter of John Barrymore (billed as "The World's Greatest Actor" in his heyday in the 1920s), great-niece of stage actors Lionel and Ethel Barrymore, and daughter of movie actor John Drew Barrymore—"wild child" Drew Barrymore has appeared in many films, including "Batman Forever" (1995), "Charlie's Angels" (2000) and the follow-up "Charlie's Angels: Full Throttle" (2003), and "Confessions Of A Dangerous Mind" (2002).

Alan Bates

British actor Alan Bates (born 1934, died 2003) accepts the Tony for best performance by a leading actor in a play for his role in "Fortune's Fool," during the 56th annual Tony Awards June 2, 2002, at New York's Radio City Music Hall. Sir Alan (he was knighted in 2003) was an acclaimed stage actor and appeared in international hit movies such as "Whistle Down The Wind" (1961), "The Fixer" (1966), for which he was nominated for an Academy Award for Best Actor in a Leading Role, "Georgy Girl" (1966), and as the butler in "Gosford Park" (2001). (AP Photo via EMPICS)

Kim Basinger

Former model Kim Basinger in New York shortly after the 1997 release of "L.A. Confidential," for which she received the Academy Award for Best Supporting Actress. She was also the star in "9½ Weeks" (1986) and "Batman" (1989). (AP Photo via EMPICS)

Kathy Bates

Playing opposite James Caan, Kathy Bates was unforgettable in "Misery" (1990), for which she received the Academy Award for Best Actress. She was also nominated for Best Actress in a Supporting Role for "About Schmidt" (2002), starring Jack Nicholson. (AP Photo via EMPICS)

Sean Bean

English actor Sean Bean is best known internationally for his performance of Boromir in the movie series "The Lord Of The Rings." He has also appeared in "Patriot Games" (1992), the Bond movie "GoldenEye" (1995), and "Flightplan" (2005), among other films, and as lead in the TV series "Sharpe."

Kate Beckinsale

Voted as among "the 100 sexiest women in the world," English actress Kate Beckinsale, star of the 2006 movie "Underworld Evolution" (sequel to the 2003 "Underworld"), appears on MTV's "Total Request Live" show at the MTV Times Square Studios, January 18, 2006, in New York. Her other major films have included box office hit "Pearl Harbor" (2001) and "The Aviator" (2004), in which latter role she played Ava Gardner. (AP Photo via EMPICS)

17

Warren Beatty

Seen here in June 2005, Warren Beatty has had nominations for Academy Awards for acting, but actually won an Oscar for directing the sprawling epic "Reds" in 1981. Brother of Shirley MacLaine, Beatty played opposite Natalie Wood in "Splendor In The Grass" (1961) and won critical acclaim as producer of and star in "Bonnie And Clyde" (1967) and "Bugsy" (1991).

Ingrid Bergman

Swedish-born actress Ingrid Bergman, shown in 1957, won her first Academy Award for Best Actress in 1944 for "Gaslight," her second in 1956, again as Best Actress, for "Anastasia," and her third, for Best Supporting Actress in 1974, for "Murder On The Orient Express." She played opposite Humphrey Bogart in one of the most romantic partnerships in movie history in "Casablanca" (1942). She died at age 67 in 1982. (AP Photo via EMPICS)

Halle Berry

Born in Cleveland, Ohio, in 1966, Halle Berry (seen here in 2005) won the Academy Award for Best Actress in 2002—the first African American to do so—for her role in "Monster's Ball," weeping unforgettably during her acceptance speech. She also starred in the Bond movie "Die Another Day" (2002) and "Catwoman" (2004).

Dirk Bogarde

The suave British actor Dirk Bogarde, knighted in 1992 for his services to acting, is best remembered internationally for his performances in "The Servant" (1963), "The Damned" (1969), "Death In Venice" (1970), and "The Night Porter" (1974). His real name was Derek Jules Gaspard Ulric Niven van den Bogaerde. He died aged 78 in 1999. (AP Photo via EMPICS)

Humphrey Bogart

Within five years during the 1940s, Humphrey Bogart emerged not just as a great film star but as one of the legends of the cinema. Formerly having generally played cynical, tough gangsters, he was cast as the good guy, the hero, first in "The Maltese Falcon" (1944), then in "Casablanca" (he's shown here with Ingrid Bergman in a scene from the 1942 classic), "To Have And Have Not," and "The Big Sleep" 1946. A mix of roles followed, with him displaying his Oscar-winning acting skills, including "The African Queen" (1951) and "The Caine Mutiny" (1954). (AP Photo via EMPICS)

Helena Bonham Carter

From an aristocratic family (including former British Prime Minister Herbert Henry Asquith), and previously best known for her performances in costume dramas (such as "Lady Jane" and "A Room With A View," both 1986), English actress Helena Bonham Carter has more recently enhanced her profile in wider-range acting and animation-voice parts such as in "Fight Club" (1999), "Charlie And The Chocolate Factory" (2005), "Corpse Bride" (voice, 2005), and "Wallace & Gromit: The Curse Of The Were-Rabbit" (voice again, 2005).

Kenneth Branagh

British Shakespearean actor, movie star and director Kenneth Branagh arrives at the world premiere of the film "Harry Potter And The Chamber Of Secrets," in which he played Professor Gilderoy Lockhart, in London November 3, 2002. His most critically acclaimed performance was as the title role in "Henry V" (1989), for which he was nominated for an Academy Award for Best Actor, and also for Best Director. (AP Photo via EMPICS)

Marlon Brando

Oscar winner for his role as Mafia boss Don Corleone in "The Godfather" (1971), and magnificent in the erotic "Last Tango In Paris" (1972), Marlon Brando learned his Stanislavsky "method" acting style in the 1940s and used it to great effect in such classic movies as "A Streetcar Named Desire" (1951) and "On The Waterfront" (1954), for which he was awarded his first Oscar. Influential and controversial, he died in 2004 aged 80. (AP Photo via EMPICS)

Jeff Bridges

Hailing from a movie-star family (son of Lloyd, brother of Beau, uncle to Jordan), Jeff Bridges has been nominated for Academy Awards for acting four times. His films have included "The Last Picture Show" (1971), "Thunderbolt And Lightfoot" (1974), and "The Contender" (2000).

Charles Bronson

Born Charles Dennis Buchinsky in Pennsylvania in 1921, tough-guy actor Charles Bronson appeared in many successful films such as "The Magnificent Seven" (1960), "The Great Escape" (1963), and "The Dirty Dozen" (1967) before becoming a box office star in his own right with the controversial vigilante movie "Death Wish" (1974) which was followed by several sequels. He died, aged 81, in 2003. (AP Photo via EMPICS)

Pierce Brosnan

Irish-born actor and producer Pierce Brosnan starred in four Bond films ("GoldenEye," "Tomorrow Never Dies," "The World Is Not Enough," and "Die Another Day") between 1995 and 2002. Throughout his Bond career, he appeared in many other films, and has since received critical praise for his performance in the comedy drama "The Matador" (2005). (AP Photo via EMPICS)

Yul Brynner

Yul Brynner's fame as a movie star basically emanates from his arrogant persona and bald head displayed in two films, the musical "The King And I" (1956), for which he won an Academy Award for Best Actor, and the Western "The Magnificent Seven" (1960). Russian by birth (in 1915), he appeared in many other films, including historical epics, and died in 1985.

Richard Burton

Richard Burton and Elizabeth Taylor attend a function during a visit to Rome, Italy, in March 1966. Welshman Burton's screen performances have been generally regarded as either good ("Look Back In Anger" in 1958) or mediocre ("The Robe" in 1953). Despite his having been nominated for Oscars seven times, his career appears to have been overshadowed by his tempestuous relationship with Taylor, whom he married twice. He died at age 58 in 1984. (AP Photo via EMPICS)

James Caan

Despite not having been typecast during a career lasting more than four decades, James Caan (seen here in 2005) has performed well in a variety of movies in which either he or those around him suffer dreadfully (witness "The Godfather" in 1972, "Rollerball" and "The Killer Elite" in 1975, and of course "Misery" in 1990). These and others of his films are eminently watchable. (AP Photo via EMPICS)

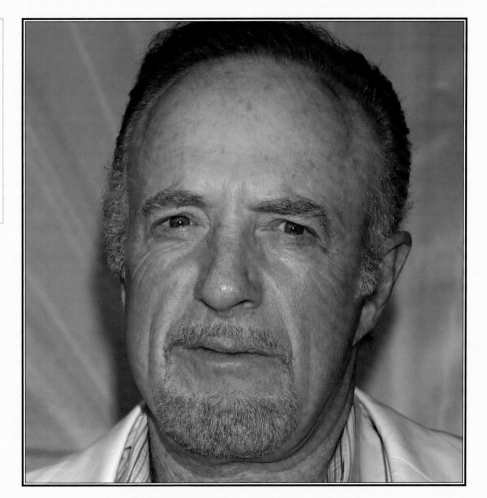

Nicholas Cage

Nicholas Cage arrives at the New York premiere of the film "The Weather Man," in which he stars, October 24, 2005. Born Nicholas Kim Coppola in California in 1964, Cage is a nephew of film director and screenwriter Francis Ford Coppola. He has played a wide range of parts in many internationally successful movies, including "Leaving Las Vegas" (1995), for which he was awarded an Oscar for Best Actor, "Gone In Sixty Seconds" (2000), and "Captain Corelli's Mandolin" (2001). (AP Photo via EMPICS)

James Cagney

Cinema's greatest gangster, James Cagney was always the tough guy, seeming always to be on the balls of his feet, delivering dialog staccato-style, even in lighthearted roles such as in the 1933 "Footlight Parade." He was a thoroughly professional, accomplished actor and dancer who will always be remembered for "Public Enemy" (1931), which launched him into stardom, "Angels With Dirty Faces" (1938), and "Yankee Doodle Dandy" (1942) for which he was awarded an Oscar for Best Actor. Here, he is shown as a crusading reporter in the 1943 film, "Johnny Come Lately." He died at age 86 in 1986.

Michael Caine

Ironically, although he became known as a chirpy London cockney in "Alfie" (1966), Michael Caine's breakthrough role was as an aristocratic officer in "Zulu" (1964). The talented British actor of prodigious output has appeared in many box office successes, including the movie that made him an international star, "The Ipcress File" (1965), "Educating Rita" (1983), and two films for which he was awarded Oscars for Best Supporting Actor, "Hannah And Her Sisters" (1986) and "The Cider House Rules" (1999). (AP Photo via EMPICS))

Jim Carrey

Canadian-born comedy actor Jim Carrey interacts
with the audience at the 2000 MTV Video Music
Awards, at Radio City Music Hall in New York,
September 2000. He appeared in "Batman Forever"
in 1995, but became a hit in the critically derided
but commercially successful "Ace Ventura, Pet
Detective" in 1994, and starred in the better-
received "Liar Liar" in 1997 and "Eternal Sunshine
Of The Spotless Mind" in 2004. (AP Photo via
EMPICS)

David Carradine

Hailing from a family of actors, David Carradine
strikes a martial arts pose at his home in Los
Angeles, March 10, 2004. Carradine is best known
for his starring roles in the "Kung Fu" movie (and
TV) series between the 1970s and 1990s, and in the
violent 2003-2004 "Kill Bill Vol. 1" and "Kill Bill
Vol. 2" written and directed by Quentin Tarantino.
(AP Photo via EMPICS)

Jackie Chan

Hong Kong Chinese acrobatic martial arts protagonist, actor, director and stuntman Jackie Chan (seen here in 1980) is best known for his high-action "Kung Fu fighting" roles. He has made more than 100 films since the 1960s, but his U.S. box office breakthrough did not come until "Rumble In The Bronx" in 1994. Chan has also enjoyed a successful music career and sings many of the theme songs in his films.

HARTSOOK
PHOT.
S.F.-LA.

Charlie Chaplin

One of the most famous movie stars of all time, British-born Charlie Chaplin (seen here in 1914) had a film persona made up of an odd mix of the humorous, sassy, ornery, obstreperous down-and-out who was always pitted against authority. His performance in "Tillie's Punctured Romance" (1914) put him on the road to fame, but his first masterpiece among many was "The Tramp" (1915). He stayed silent in his movies through the 1930s, making his first talkie, the Hitler-lampooning "The Great Dictator," in 1940. Chaplin was awarded two honorary Oscars over forty years apart, for "The Circus" in 1929, and in 1972 for his contribution to motion pictures, and also received an Academy Award in 1973 for Best Music in an Original Classic Score for the 1952 film "Limelight." A long-time controversial figure, Chaplin was knighted by Britain's Queen Elizabeth II in 1975, and died in Switzerland in 1977 at age 88.

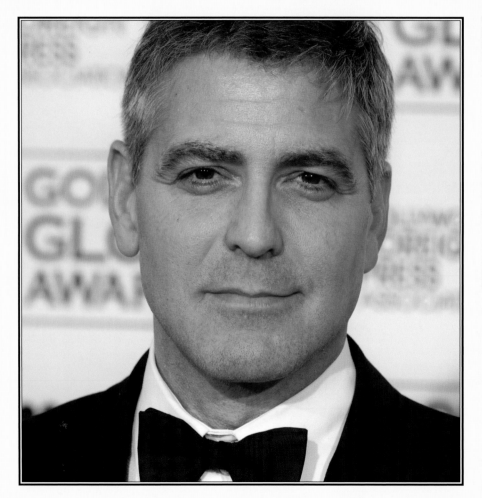

George Clooney

Heartthrob actor and movie director George Clooney was already famous for his role in the TV hospital drama "E/R" when his film career really took off in "The Perfect Storm" in 2000, followed up with such successes as "Ocean's Eleven" (2001), "Welcome To Collinwood" (2002), and "Intolerable Cruelty" (2003), and in 2006 won the Oscar for Best Supporting Actor for his part in "Syriana." He directed "Confessions Of A Dangerous Mind" in 2002 and "Good Night, And Good Luck" (which he co-wrote and starred in) in 2005. (He is also nephew of actress and singer Rosemary Clooney.)

Glenn Close

Glenn Close attends the world premiere of "Hoodwinked," December 3, 2005, in New York. She has played scheming and chilling roles in "Fatal Attraction" (1987), "Dangerous Liaisons" (1988), and "101 Dalmations" (1996), in which she gives a deliciously evil, over-the-top performance as Cruella de Vil. Close is also an acclaimed stage actress, one of her roles being Norma Desmond in the Andrew Lloyd Webber musical "Sunset Boulevard." Fans are looking forward to her appearance in the movie version. (AP Photo via EMPICS)

Claudette Colbert

Born in Paris, France, in 1905, but definitely an American actress who appeared in more than sixty films, Claudette Colbert is shown in costume for the title role in "Zaza" in 1938. She was a brilliant comedy actress, as epitomized in her best movies, notably opposite Clark Gable in "It Happened One Night" (1934), for which she received a Best Actress Oscar, and with Fred MacMurray in "The Gilded Lily" (1935). She died in Barbados in 1996 at age 92. (AP Photo via EMPICS)

Robert Colman

Swiss politician Marcel Pilet-Golaz, right, and his wife visit actor Ronald Colman on the set of Colman's picture, "The Late George Apley," in Hollywood, July 10, 1946. A distinguished, romantic figure, English-born Colman was one of the few top silent movie actors to become an even bigger talkie star. In 1947 he won the Best Actor Oscar for his role in "A Double Life." (AP Photo via EMPICS)

Sean Connery

The first, and arguably the best, 007 in seven of the James Bond series of movies, Scottish-born Sean Connery carved out a successful post-Bond career, notably for his tough-cop role in "The Untouchables" (1987), for which he received an Academy Award for Best Supporting Actor, and the Cold War drama "The Hunt For Red October" (1990). He was knighted in 2000. (AP Photo via EMPICS)

Gary Cooper

Regarded as one of the half-dozen greatest movie stars, Gary Cooper had a screen persona as the slow-speaking, deep-thinking, and utterly determined man of integrity, epitomized in his performances in "Sergeant York" (1941) and "High Noon" (1952), for both of which roles he received Best Actor Academy Awards. Here he is seen with Joan Fontaine, February 27, 1942. (Fontaine won Best Actress Award for her role in "Suspicion.") Cooper was born of English parents in Montana in 1901 and died in 1961. (AP Photo via EMPICS)

Kevin Costner

One of his best films was the political thriller, "No Way Out" (1987), but Kevin Costner is best known for starring in and directing "Dances With Wolves" (1990), awarded Oscars for Best Picture and Best Director. Costner and his girlfriend Christine Baumgartner are shown in this photo taken by a friend during a visit to Aspen, Co., in early 2003. (AP Photo via EMPICS)

41

Joan Crawford

"I love to play bitches," Joan Crawford once said, and she often lived up to that on-screen and, apparently, off. She frequently played (and lived) as a tough, shrewd, determined woman, none more so than in "Mildred Pierce" (1945), for which she won a Best Actress Oscar. Born Lucille Fay LeSueur in Texas in 1905, she adopted a fixed, determine look, with broad mouth and arched eyebrows, and made more than eighty films from the silent era through to 1970. She died in 1977.
(AP Photo via EMPICS)

Bing Crosby

One of the most popular American entertainers of the 20th century, relaxed crooner Bing Crosby was a better actor than many acknowledged, winning an Oscar for Best Actor in "Going My Way" (1944) and singing four Academy Award-winning songs, including the incredibly enduring "White Christmas" in the film of the same name (1954). Here, Crosby and Bob Hope enjoy a smoke from a water pipe on March 30, 1962, in a scene from "The Road to Hong Kong." (AP Photo via EMPICS)

Russell Crowe

Temperamental superstar Russell Crowe was born in New Zealand in 1964 and has notched up huge box office hits with "L.A. Confidential" (1997), "The Insider" (1999), "Gladiator" (2000), for which he was awarded Best Actor Oscar, and "A Beautiful Mind" (2001). Here, he smiles at the premiere of his 2005 film "Cinderella Man."

Tom Cruise

Fighter pilot (in "Top Gun," 1986); paralyzed Vietnam War veteran and anti-war activist (in "Born On The Fourth Of July," 1989); military lawyer (in "A Few Good Men," 1992); secret agent (in 1996-2006 "Mission: Impossible" series); sports agent (in "Jerry Maguire," 1996); sexual adventurer (in "Eyes Wide Shut," 1999)—superstar Tom Cruise has played a wide variety of roles in movies that have mainly been massive earners at the box office. (AP Photo via EMPICS)

Billy Crystal

TV star, movie actor and producer Billy Crystal has enjoyed a warm appreciation among cinema audiences, particularly for the comedies "Throw Mother From The Train" (1987), "When Harry Met Sally...." (1989), and "Analyze This" (1999) with Robert De Niro.

Jamie Lee Curtis

Daughter of Tony Curtis and Janet Leigh, Jamie Lee Curtis has assumed a variety of film roles, from dramatic to comic, and is especially known for her appearance in the "Halloween" series of movies that have been released between 1978 and 2002. (AP Photo via EMPICS)

Tony Curtis

Lampooned for his delivery (in inimitable Bronx accent) of the line "Yonder lies da castle of my fahder" as an English knight in "The Black Shield of Falworth" (1954), Tony Curtis has nevertheless proven himself a fine actor, having made more than 100 films, most notably "The Defiant Ones" (1958), the excellent "Sweet Smell Of Success" (1957), and the funny "Some Like It Hot" (1959). Six-times married Curtis is the father of actresses Jamie Lee Curtis and Kelly Curtis. (AP Photo via EMPICS)

John Cusack

Actors John Cusack, top, and Bret Loehr, kid around before a screening of "Identity" in Los Angeles, April, 23, 2003. Cusack starred in, co-wrote and produced the comedy "Grosse Pointe Blank" (1997), and was the lead in the action drama "Con Air" (also 1997). (AP Photo via EMPICS)

Bette Davis

Bette Davis in a scene from the 1963 movie "Whatever Happened To Baby Jane?" in which she starred with Joan Crawford. Filled with ambition, Davis gritted her teeth, bulged her eyes, and succeeded in becoming one of Hollywood's greats, winning two Oscars (for "Dangerous" in 1935 and "Jezebel" in 1938) and acting memorably in the sparkling satirical comedy "All About Eve" (1950), "The Star" (1952), and "The Virgin Queen" (1955). Born in 1908, and having made close on 100 films between the 1930s and the 1980s, she died in 1989.
(AP Photo via EMPICS)

Doris Day

Accomplished comedienne and singer Doris Day enjoyed her heyday in the 1950s and 1960s, when she was probably the top box office draw of them all, exploiting a wholesome but alluring image in such successes as "Calamity Jane" (1953), "Love Me Or Leave Me" (1955), and "Pillow Talk" (1959). Here, she is shown at the witness stand after obtaining a divorce from her second husband, musician George Weidler, at the Los Angeles County Superior Court, May 31, 1949. She married twice more, her third husband, Marty Melcher, apparently squandering her earnings to the extent that she was bankrupt when he died in 1968. (AP Photo via EMPICS)

Daniel Day-Lewis

English/Irish Daniel Day-Lewis received the Academy Award as Best Actor for his wheelchair-bound role in the 1989 film "My Left Foot," and achieved further acclaim for his performances in "The Last Of The Mohicans" (1992), "The Crucible" (1996), and "Gangs Of New York" (2002). He is notorious for his intense attention to detail and preparation for his roles, and for frequently refusing to come out of character during the production of his films.

Olivia de Havilland

In the 1930s, Olivia de Havilland played opposite Errrol Flynn in the swashbuckling movies "Captain Blood" and "The Adventures Of Robin Hood," but also was awarded an Oscar (for Best Supporting Actress) in 1939 for her appearance in "Gone With The Wind" (1939). She went on to win an Oscar for Best Actress for "To Each His Own" (1946), and another for "The Heiress" (1949). The photo shows her in a period costume from the 1958 movie "The Proud Rebel." (AP Photo via EMPICS)

Robert De Niro

One of the finest actors throughout the last thirty years, Robert De Niro is shown in a scene from the 1980 Martin Scorsese film "Raging Bull," for which De Niro was awarded the Oscar for Best Actor. His relationship with Scorsese spawned many oyher great movies, including "Taxi Driver" (1976), "Goodfellas" (1990), "Cape Fear" (1991), and "Casino" (1995). De Niro received another Academy Award (Best Supporting Actor) for his part in "The Godfather, Part II," and further displayed his versatility in comedies such as "Analyze This," (1999), "Meet The Parents" (2000), and "Analyze That" (2002). (AP Photo via EMPICS)

James Dean

Born in 1931, James Dean built a screen persona in two 1955 films: "East Of Eden," in which he played a young man craving for his parents' understanding; and "Rebel Without A Cause," as an anguished son crying out against adult insensitivity. The persona was further shaped for public adulation by his directors and, following the 1956 movie "Giant," death turned Dean into a legend: he died in 1955 the day after the film's completion when he crashed in his new Porsche 550 Spyder. The photo shows Dean as Jim Stark in a scene from "Rebel Without A Cause." (AP Photo via EMPICS)

Judi Dench

English stage, TV, and film actress Dame Judi Dench arrives for a Royal Film Performance of her movie "Ladies In Lavender" in London, November 8, 2004. Nominated several times for Academy Awards, she won the 1999 Oscar for Best Supporting Actress for her performance in "Shakespeare In Love." Her range has been proven in a wide variety of box-office successes, from Queen Victoria in "Mrs. Brown" (1997) to her lead in "Iris" (2001), in which she portrayed the novelist Iris Murdoch suffering from Alzheimer's disease.

Johnny Depp

Nominated for Academy Awards for Best Actor in "Pirates Of The Caribbean: The Curse Of The Black Pearl" (2004) and "Finding Neverland" (2005), Johnny Depp is famed for his wide variety of roles, such as the artificial man "Edward Scissorhands" (1990) and as Willy Wonka in "Charlie And The Chocolate Factory" (2005).

Danny DeVito

Talented actor, director, and producer Danny DeVito and former acting co-star (now Governor of California) Arnold Schwarzenegger strike poses on the set of De Vito's movie "Relative Strangers," October 13, 2004. DeVito directed and appeared in the Michael Douglas/Kathleen Turner smash hit dark comedy "The War Of The Roses" (1989), was particularly memorable co-starring with Richard Dreyfuss in the comedy "Tin Men" (1987), and portrayed the villain The Penguin in "Batman Returns" (1992). (AP Photo via EMPICS)

Leonardo DiCaprio

Having been launched from stardom in "Romeo + Juliet," in 1996, into superstardom with his starring role in "Titanic" (1997), Leonardo DiCaprio has furthered his movie career under top directors Steven Spielberg ("Catch Me If You Can," 2002) and Martin Scorsese ("Gangs Of New York," 2002, and "The Aviator," 2004). (AP Photo via EMPICS)

Marlene Dietrich

From being one of the top international movie stars of the early 1930s (witness her starring role in the 1930 "The Blue Angel," ever-remembered for the song "Falling In Love Again"), German-born singer and actress Marlene Dietrich saw her career virtually collapse by 1936. But she made one of several successful comebacks in "Destry Rides Again" (1939), opposite James Stewart, that kept her in movies for decades, her final appearance in a film being in "Just A Gigolo" (1979) with rock star David Bowie. She died at age 90 in 1992.

Kirk Douglas

Kirk Douglas clenched his teeth, honed his body, and thrust his cleft chin to the fore as he fought tooth and nail to become a great movie star throughout the 1950s and early 1960s. He displayed versatility in many films, including as an ambitious reporter in "Ace In The Hole" (1951), as Vincent Van Gough in "Lust For Life" (1956), as Doc Holiday in "Gunfight At The OK Corral" (1957), as disillusioned World War I French army officer in perhaps his finest role in "Paths Of Glory" (1957), and as idealist gladiator in the epic "Spartacus" (1960). He was honored with a special Oscar in 1996, the same year that he suffered a debilitating stroke. The photo shows him in 2001, shortly before his 85th birthday. One of his four sons is Michael Douglas. (AP Photo via EMPICS)

Michael Douglas

Following in the footsteps of his father, Kirk, Michael Douglas has emerged as one of the great movie stars of the modern era, displaying his versatility in, among other box-office hits, his acting breakthrough in "Romancing The Stone" (1984), "Fatal Attraction" (1987), "The War Of The Roses" (1989), and "Basic Instinct" (2002). He received an Academy Award for Best Actor for "Wall Street" (1988), and has also produced several films, winning an Oscar for "One Flew Over The Cuckoo's Nest" (1975). He is married to Catherine Zeta-Jones. (AP Photo via EMPICS)

Richard Dreyfuss

Richard Dreyfuss built a screen reputation playing introverted obsessives (focusing on sharks in "Jaws," 1975, and on flying saucers in "Close Encounters Of The Third Kind," 1977). He was brilliant as a worried actor in "The Goodbye Girl" (1977), for which he won the Oscar for Best Actor, at the time the youngest actor (at age 30) ever to do so. His career dipped in the early 1980s, but his versatility saw him bounce back in "Down And Out In Beverley Hills" in 1986. (AP Photo via EMPICS)

Minnie Driver

British actress and singer/songwriter Minnie Driver ironically had her voice dubbed in songs in the 2004 movie "The Phantom Of The Opera." She made her breakthrough with her starring role in the film of Maeve Binchy's novel, "Circle Of Friends" (1995) and has had major parts in many other films, including "Good Will Hunting" (1997).

Robert Duvall

Critically acclaimed actor and director Robert Duvall has a tremendous list of credits, including his movie debut in "To Kill A Mockingbird" (1962), "The Godfather" (1972), "The Godfather Part II" (1974), and "Apocalypse Now" (1979), but it was for his performance as an alcoholic country music singer in "Tender Mercies" (1983) that he received the Academy Award for Best Actor. (AP Photo via EMPICS)

Clint Eastwood

Actor, director, and producer Clint Eastwood has progressed to superstardom since his Sergio Leone "spaghetti Western" days ("A Fistful Of Dollars," etc.), through "Dirty Harry" (1971) to his acting and directing roles in "Unforgiven" (1992), "Mystic River" (2003, director-only), and "Million Dollar Baby" (2004). It's been a long road since Rowdy Yates in the TV series "Rawhide," but he appears to have nudged John Wayne off the No. 1 spot as top box office star. The photo shows him in 1967 as an unlikely captive at gunpoint at the mercy of Susan Melody (left), Sandra Marshall (center), and Anita MacGregor.

Faye Dunaway

Faye Dunaway received an Academy Award for Best Actress in the 1977 movie "Network." She had been nominated twice before, as Best Actress in her breakthrough film "Bonnie And Clyde" (1967) with Warren Beatty, and "Chinatown" (1974) opposite Jack Nicholson. She has not been able to repeat such successes even though she gave creditable performances in many films, including "Mommie Dearest" (1981), in which she played Joan Crawford, "Barfly" (1987) opposite Mickey Rourke, and "Don Juan DeMarco" (1995), which also starred Johnny Depp and Marlon Brando.

English stage actor Albert Finney had his first starring role in the movies as the working class hero in "Saturday Night And Sunday Morning" (1960, see photo) and followed up with the box office success "Tom Jones" (1963), but his most famous part was as Belgian detective Hercule Poirot in the film of Agatha Christie's novel "Murder On The Orient Express" (1974). Though he felt typecast by that role for many years, he has since played well in supporting roles such as in "Annie" (1982) and "Erin Brockovich" (2000). (AP Photo via EMPICS)

Errol Flynn

The best devil-may-care swashbuckler of the 1930s (in "Captain Blood," 1935, and "The Adventures Of Robin Hood," 1938) who then went on to practically win the war for America in the 1940s, Australian/American Errol Flynn was a better screen actor than many give him credit for. Among scores of films he made, good ones included "They Died With Their Boots On" (1941), in which he played General Custer, and "Gentleman Jim" (1942), as heavyweight boxing champion Jim Corbett. Here, he is shown with his pet schnauzer Moody while the actor rests on his canvas chair on the set of "Never Say Goodbye" in August 1945. Born in 1909, he died at age 50 in 1959. (AP Photo via EMPICS)

Ralph Fiennes

The much-lauded English stage actor Ralph Fiennes had his screen debut in 1992 as Heathcliff in "Wuthering Heights," but achieved international fame for his role as Nazi concentration camp commandant in "Schindler's List" (1993) and as lead in "The English Patient" (1996), for both of which performances he was nominated for Oscars (Best Supporting Actor and Best Actor, respectively). In 2005 he appeared as the evil Lord Voldemort in the fourth Harry Potter film, and as the star in "The Constant Gardener."

Henry Fonda

In a career lasting almost fifty years playing such widely disparate roles as honest, idealistic hero ("Young Mr. Lincoln" in 1939) and ruthless killer (in Sergio Leone's "Once Upon A Time In The West" in 1968), Henry Fonda was a great screen actor who received an Honorary Academy Award in 1981 and Best Actor Oscar for "On Golden Pond" (1982), which also starred his daughter Jane and Katherine Hepburn. His finest films were the pioneer-life "My Darling Clementine" (1946) and courtroom drama "Twelve Angry Men" (1957). Married five times, Fonda led a dynasty of actors— son Peter, daughter Jane, granddaughter Bridget, and grandson Troy Garity. He died in 1982. Here, he is shown rehearsing a scene as General Douglas MacArthur in the TV movie "Collision Course" in 1975. (AP Photo via EMPICS)

Glenn Ford

Canadian-born Glenn Ford adopted a screen persona that combined relaxed amiability with determination, and showed his fine acting ability in romantic dramas such as "Gilda" (1946) with Rita Hayworth, comedies such as "A Pocketful Of Miracles" (1961) with Hope Lange and Bette Davis, and action movies such as "The Big Heat" (1953) with Gloria Grahame. Born in 1916, he was making films for the big screen and TV as late as 1991. The photo shows him in 1947 in costume for his role in the movie "The Loves of Carmen," sitting on the motorcycle he rode to and from location "rather than a horse." (AP Photo via EMPICS)

Harrison Ford

One of the highest box office earners in history, Harrison Ford has played high-profile roles in both the "Star Wars" and "Indiana Jones" series (between 1977 and 1993), as well as the leads in such films as "Witness" (1985), "Patriot Games" (1992), "Clear And Present Danger" (1994), and "What Lies Beneath" (2000). Apparently, Indiana Jones will be reprised in 2007. (AP Photo via EMPICS)

Jodie Foster

Having made a successful transition from child to adult
star, Jodie Foster has also survived rough treatment as a
gang-rape victim in "The Accused" (1988) and
encounters with Hannibal Lecter in "The Silence Of
The Lambs" (1991), for both of which she received
Academy Awards for Best Actress. After that, her role in
"Flightplan" (2005) as the mother of a daughter who
goes missing during a transatlantic flight holds a
different form of terror. Surely real-life Jodie can
cope....After all, she's made more than a hundred TV
and film appearances since she was five years of age, is an
accomplished director and producer, has performed in
French language films, and even been stalked by the
would-be assassin of President Ronald Reagan in 1981.
(AP Photo via EMPICS)

Morgan Freeman

In 2005 Morgan Freeman received the Academy Award
for Best Supporting Actor in Clint Eastwood's "Million
Dollar Baby," and has won international acclaim for his
performances in "Driving Miss Daisy" (1989) and "The
Shawshank Redemption" (1994) among other high-
profile movies. His rich, smooth voice has been heard in
voice-overs, too, as in the narration of "War Of The
Worlds" and "March Of The Penguins" (both 2005).

Clark Gable

"I can't act worth a damn," Clark Gable once said. A lot of people would agree, but nevertheless Gable, whom Joan Crawford called the King of Hollywood, made some hugely successful films, including his biggest seller, "Gone With The Wind" (1939). Although he won the Academy Award for Best Actor in "It Happened One Night" (1934), his best performance (and his last) was probably in "The Misfits" (1960) with Marilyn Monroe. He died a few weeks after finishing it, in his sixtieth year. The photo shows him with frequent co-star Jean Harlow.

Greta Garbo

Although she appeared in only three silent films in Europe, ten silent films in Hollywood, and fourteen American sound films, Swedish-born Greta Garbo was probably the most adulated movie star of the late 1920s and 1930s. Her personality was a major part of her image, her shyness making her withdrawn and apparently aloof, epitomized by her catchphrase, "I want to be alone." Her best film was "Queen Christina" (1933) and her last "Two-Faced Woman" (1941). The photo shows her as she appeared in the role of "Mata Hari" in 1931. She died in 1990 at age 84. (AP Photo via EMPICS)

Ava Gardner

Ava Gardner (born 1922, died 1990) was one of those great movie stars whose off-screen image seemed intermingled with and reflected in her on-screen personality, and vice versa. Her image was that of the independent-minded, worldly-wise beauty who fascinated men and worried wives. Born poor, she became the restless playgirl involved with James Mason in "Pandora And The Flying Dutchman" (1951) and the sensual, temperamental beauty built to stardom in "The Barefoot Contessa" (1954). Her image seemed particularly right in Africa with Clark Gable in "Mogambo" (1953) and again with Stewart Granger in "Bhowani Junction" (1956). At nineteen she was married briefly to Mickey Rooney, then to jazz musician Artie Shaw, then to Frank Sinatra, and had highly publicized affairs with Howard Hughes and George C. Scott.

James Garner

One of the most engaging, easy-going personalities in cinema, James Garner has played several parts calling for a slightly bumbling, reluctant hero who ultimately copes with courage and competence when absolutely required: witness "The Great Escape" (1963) in which he was the PoW scrounger able to barter or steal anything required by the escape committee; "The Americanization Of Emily" (1964), in which he was a World War II officer forced to become a D-Day hero; and "Support Your Local Sheriff" (1968), taming toughs in a Wild West boom town. In real life he was awarded the Purple Heart during the Korean War. Garner has also enjoyed a major TV career, particularly in the "Maverick" and "The Rockford Files" series. (AP Photo via EMPICS)

Richard Gere

Once voted "the sexiest man alive," Richard Gere has appeared in many box office successes, including his breakthrough movie "American Gigolo" (1980), "An Officer And A Gentleman" (1982), "Pretty Woman" (1990), and "Chicago" (2002). Politically active, Gere is shown addressing a London crowd against apartheid and in support of Nelson Mandela, during a 70th birthday tribute to the jailed ANC leader (and subsequent South African president) in 1988. (AP Photo via EMPICS)

Mel Gibson

Although Mel Gibson was born in New York he was raised in Australia. Conversely, although his 1979 debut movie "Mad Max" was made in Australia, his sequels to it were made in the U.S. His first American screen appearance was as Fletcher Christian in "The Bounty" (1984), and he has risen to box office stardom in such hits as the 1987-1998 "Lethal Weapon" series, "Braveheart" (1995), which won Oscars for Best Director and Best Picture, "What Women Want" (2000), while he co-wrote, produced and directed the controversial 2004 movie "The Passion Of The Christ." (AP Photo via EMPICS)

Whoopi Goldbebrg

Stand-up comedienne, actress and singer Whoopi Goldberg was born Caryn Elaine Johnson in 1955 and made her movie debut in Steven Spielberg's "The Color Purple" (1985). She has gone on to achieve critical acclaim in "Jumpin' Jack Flash" (1986), "Ghost" (1990), for which she received the Academy Award for Best Supporting Actress, and "Sister Act" (1991), while appearing in "Star Trek" films on the big screen and TV.

Betty Grable

"The girl with the million-dollar legs," Betty Grable was the GIs' pin-up girl in World War II and a top box office draw from 1942 to 1951, during which time she appeared in popular musicals such as "Coney Island" and "Sweet Rosie O'Grady" in 1943, "The Dolly Sisters" (1946), and "Mother Wore Tights" (1947). She was effectively ousted by Marilyn Monroe in "How To Marry A Millionaire" (1953), which featured both of them. Grable is shown with new husband Jackie Coogan cutting their wedding cake in 1937. She died in 1973 at age 57. (AP Photo via EMPICS)

Alec Guinness

A truly great English actor in superb dramas ("Great Expectations" in 1946 and "Oliver Twist" in 1948) as well as comedies ("The Lavender Hill Mob" in 1951 and "The Lady Killers" in 1955), Alec Guinness attained international stardom in "The Bridge On The River Kwai" in 1957, for which he received the Academy Award for Best Actor. Twenty years later he began featuring as Obi-Wan Kenobi in the "Star Wars" series, and appeared in many more fine films. The photo shows him during the filming of "The Bridge On The River Kwai." Knighted in 1959, Sir Alec died in 2000 at age 86. (AP Photo via EMPICS)

Cary Grant

British-born Cary Grant was a movie natural, always charming and debonair but exceedingly masculine, his critics rarely giving him due credit for actually acting (he never won an Oscar for Best Actor, although he did receive an Academy Award for Lifetime Achievement in 1970). His consummate timing made him a favorite of Alfred Hitchcock, in whose "To Catch A Thief" (1955) and "North By Northwest" (1959) he starred. He also appeared as lead in director Howard Hawks' films, including "Bringing Up Baby" (1938) and "Only Angels Have Wings" (1939). Grant appeared opposite many of the great female stars including Mae West, Jean Harlow, Joan Fontaine, Ingrid Bergman, Grace Kelly, Sophia Loren, Audrey Hepburn, and Katherine Hepburn. He died in 1986 at the age of 82.

Gene Hackman

Gene Hackman won the 1971 Academy Award for Best Actor for his portrayal of the dogged, grim, and violent narcotics detective Popeye Doyle in "The French Connection," which made him a star. Born in 1930, Hackman has played the tough guy in other good movies such as "Night Moves" (1975), "The Domino Principle" (1977), and "Unforgiven" (1992), which earned him another Oscar (for Best Supporting Actor). However, it was his performances as the distressed son in "I Never Sang For My Father" (1969) and the over-involved surveillance expert in "The Conversation" (1974) that proved his fine acting ability. The photo shows him (at left) with co-star Ben Stiller at the premiere of the comedy drama "The Royal Tenenbaums" in 2001. (AP Photo via EMPICS)

Tom Hanks

Born in 1956, Tom Hanks has become a most versatile and important box office movie star since his debut film "He Knows You're Alone" in 1980. His fine films displaying great, wide-ranging acting ability have included "Big" (1988), "Sleepless In Seattle" (1993), "Philadelphia" (1993), for which he received the Academy Award for Best Actor, "Forrest Gump" (1994), winning him another Best Actor Oscar, "Saving Private Ryan" (1998), "The Green Mile" (1999), and "Road To Perdition" (2002). The photo shows him waving Elizabeth Taylor's speech that she was to read before presenting the Hollywood Outstanding Achievement in Songwriting Award to Carol Bayer Sager in 2002. In Taylor's absence Hanks presented the award. (AP Photo via EMPICS)

Jean Harlow

With a screen persona that was tough, wise-cracking, somewhat slatternly and sexually voracious, Jean Harlow—the "platinum blonde" who wore clinging satin dresses without a bra—was very much the sex symbol of the 1930s. She was the perfect screen partner for leading men such as Ben Lyon (to whom she uttered the immortal "Pardon me while I slip into something more comfortable" in her first starring role in the 1930 "Hells Angels"), James Cagney, and Clark Gable. She appeared in dramas and comedies (even with Laurel and Hardy) right through to the last film she was to complete, "Personal Property" with Robert Taylor in 1937. The same year she was making "Saratoga" with Gable when she became ill with kidney failure and died at the age of 26. (AP Photo via EMPICS)

Rita Hayworth

"The Great American Love Goddess" in the 1940s, redhead Rita Hayworth became famous for her part in Howard Hawks' "Only Angels Have Wings" (1939), reached her zenith in "Gilda" (1946), but fell from the throne as she moved from glamorous beauties to be cast by husband Orson Welles as the vicious wife of a cripple in "The Lady From Shanghai" (1948). She did bounce back after her 1949 marriage to Prince Aly Khan ended in 1953, but not to the top spot. An accomplished dancer, she had appeared in popular musicals, some with Gene Kelly ("Cover Girl" in 1944) and Fred Astaire ("You'll Never Get Rich" in 1941, and "You Were Never Lovelier" in 1942). When she returned to Hollywood she played opposite Frank Sinatra in "Pal Joey" and Burt Lancaster in "Separate Tables" in the late 1950s, but the sparkle had gone, the good parts dried up and, while she acted on through the next decade, it seems she showed early signs of Alzheimer's Disease that took her life in 1987 at the age of 68.

Audrey Hepburn

In the 1950s and '60s, chic and petite Belgian-born Audrey Hepburn was adored by audiences and critics alike, winning an Oscar for Best Actress in her first starring role, opposite Gregory Peck, in "Roman Holiday" (1953). She played serious roles (as in the epic "War and Peace" in 1956), kookey, lighthearted parts (as in "Breakfast At Tiffany's" in 1961), and musical leads (as in "Funny Face" in 1957 and ""My Fair Lady" in 1964). She retired from the screen in 1967, but came back ten years later opposite Sean Connery in "Robin And Marion" before retiring again in 1988. She then worked tirelessly for UNICEF (United Nations Children's Fund) until cancer took her life in 1993 at the age of 63. The photo shows her as Eliza Doolittle in "My Fair Lady." (AP Photo via EMPICS)

Katherine Hepburn

With a career that lasted more than seventy years, Katherine Hepburn was regarded as one of the greatest actresses in cinema history and the recipient of four Academy Awards for Best Actress: for "Morning Glory" (1930), "Guess Who's Coming To Dinner" (1967), "The Lion In Winter" (1968), and "On Golden Pond" (1981)—and they are not even reckoned to be her best performances! These are arguably her roles in "The Philadelphia Story" (1940) and "The African Queen" (1951). Her name is forever linked with that of Spencer Tracy with whom she had an on- and off-screen relationship through nine films she made with him until his death in 1967. Hepburn (shown in 1992) died in 2003 at the age of 96.

Charlton Heston

Throughout the 1950s and '60s Charlton Heston showed he was the most popular epic star of all time through films like "Ben Hur" (for which he won the Best Actor Oscar in 1960), "The Ten Commandments," "The Greatest Show On Earth," and "El Cid," but he had already proven what a fine actor he was in smaller films such as "Ruby Gentry" in 1952 and Orson Welles' "Touch Of Evil" in 1958. He did so again when epics went out of fashion, in disaster movies like "Earthquake" (1974) and "Two Minute Warning" (1976), as well as the hugely commercial "Planet Of The Apes" (1968). (AP Photo via EMPICS)

Dustin Hoffman

Dustin Hoffman shot into the top ten of box office stars as the confused hero of "The Graduate" in 1968 and has continued to show what a fine and versatile actor he is in "Midnight Cowboy" (1969), "Papillon" (1973), "All The President's Men" (1976), "Kramer vs Kramer" (1979), for which he was awarded the Best Actor Oscar, and "Rain Man" (1988), which earned him another Oscar for Best Actor. Good at comedy too, Hoffman starred in and produced the funny "Tootsie" (1982), in which he played an actor compelled to dress as a woman to get a part in a soap opera. More recently he has appeared in dramas such as "Sleepers" (1996) and "Runaway Jury" (2003) as well as in lighthearted roles as in "Meet The Fockers" (2004). The photo shows Hoffman posing at the terrace of his hotel during the International Cannes Film Festival in 1996. (AP Photo via EMPICS)

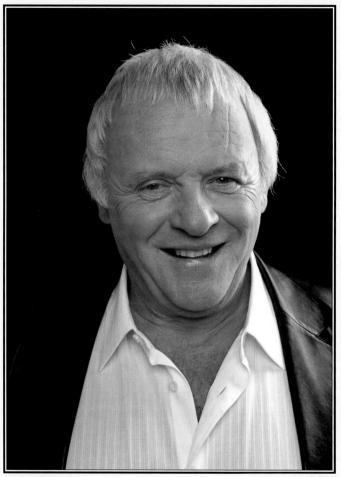

William Holden

William Holden won an Oscar for Best Actor as the guarded, maverick hero in the 1954 "Stalag 17" (see photo). He had to perform in many lesser films as a result of Hollywood contracts, but appeared brilliantly in many varied roles in successful movies such as "Sunset Boulevard" and "Born Yesterday" (both 1950), "Sabrina" (1954), "The Horse Soldiers" (1959), and "The Wild Bunch" (1969). He died in 1981 at age 63. (AP Photo via EMPICS)

Anthony Hopkins

Although Welsh-born Anthony Hopkins was on-screen for less than twenty minutes in "Silence Of The Lambs," he won the Best Actor Oscar for his portrayal of the chilling serial killer Hannibal Lecter in that 1991 box office success, then went on to reprise the role of the cannibal in "Hannibal" in 2001 and "Red Dragon" in 2002. Hopkins is best known for these films, but has displayed his wide-ranging acting prowess in many other high profile movies such as "The Bunker" (1981), "The Bounty" (1984), "The Remains Of The Day" (1993), "Nixon" (1995), and "The Mask Of Zorro" (1998). Sir Anthony was knighted in 1993. (AP Photo via EMPICS)

Rock Hudson

Rock Hudson became a top box office attraction in the 1950s and '60s through romantic melodramas (including "Magnificent Obsession" and "Written On The Wind") and bubbling sex comedies, notably with Doris Day, such as "Pillow Talk" and "Lover Come Back." Although he was an excellent light comedian, and performed well in the drama "Giant" (James Dean's last film), many critics unkindly put him down as simply a chesty leading man, and it was ironic that Hudson, who did not confirm or deny he was homosexual, died of an AIDS-related illness in 1985 at the age of 59. (AP Photo via EMPICS)

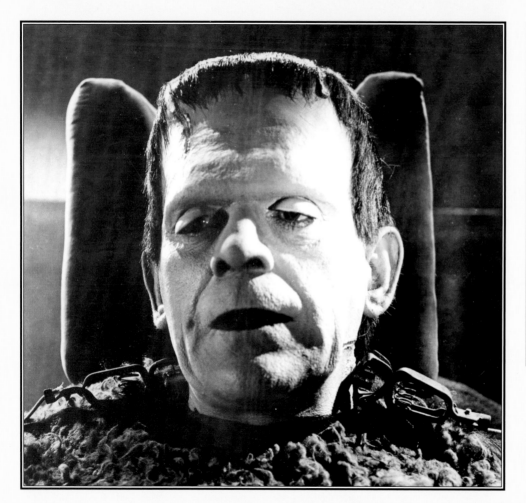

Boris Karloff

British-born Boris Karloff acted in many straight roles, but it was his work in his 1930s and '40s horror movies that made him a star. He played the monster creation in "Frankenstein" in 1931 (see photo), and in two follow-ups, so well that lesser actors in later performances of the role paled into insignificance by comparison. He starred in other classics of the horror genre such as "The Mummy" and "The Old Dark House" (both 1932) and "The Body Snatchers" in 1946, and then over twenty years later as an aging, courageous horror star in "Targets." Born in 1887, he died in 1969. (AP Photo via EMPICS)

Buster Keaton

Comic actor and director Buster Keaton was for a few years in the 1920s one of the world's greatest silent film stars. Short and dark-haired with large, sad eyes, he was nicknamed the "Great Stone Face" because of his unsmiling expression. A brilliant acrobat and stuntman, Keaton was a meticulous planner of detail: in "Steamboat Bill Jr" (1927) he allowed a whole house to collapse on him, having calculated to the inch where to stand so that a window space would fall around him. His greatest works included "The Navigator" (1924) and "The General" (1926). He did not transfer well into the "talkies," and his talents dissipated from the '30s onwards to the extent that he ended up doing bit parts and writing gags for others. He died in 1966. (AP Photo via EMPICS)

Grace Kelly

While she had appeared in "High Noon" with Gary Cooper (see photo) and "Mogambo" with Clark Gable, it was Alfred Hitchcock who made Grace Kelly a major movie star in "Dial M For Murder," "Rear Window," and "To Catch A Thief." She had the screen persona of the ice-cool princess with a suggestion of unquenchable flames, won the Oscar for Best Actress for "The Country Girl" (1954), was the daughter of a rich socialite family in "High Society" (1956), then retired to marry Prince Rainier III of Monaco having completed just eleven Hollywood films. She died following a tragic automobile accident in 1952. (AP Photo via EMPICS)

Deborah Kerr

Scottish-born Deborah Kerr developed a screen persona as a mix of refined respectability and forbidden sexuality in many of her most famous roles, such as the married nymphomaniac in a torrid affair with Burt Lancaster in "From Here To Eternity" (1953, see photo), as a nun stranded on a desert island with the leering Robert Mitchum in "Heaven Knows Mr Allison" (1957), and as a determined governess opposite Yul Brynner in the musical "The King And I" (1956). Her last major screen role was as Kirk Douglas's wife in "The Arrangement" in 1969. (AP Photo via EMPICS)

Val Kilmer

In a career spanning more than twenty years, Val Kilmer has appeared in a variety of movie roles, including rock 'n' roll star in the comedy "Top Secret," fighter pilot in "Top Gun," lead singer Jim Morrison in "The Doors," a Macedonian king in "Alexander," and as Batman in "Batman Forever." With luck his versatility will lead to a greater and longer career, and maybe Oscars.

Alan Ladd

Often cast as a killer, on either side of the law, Alan Ladd is best known for his role in the classic western "Shane" (1953) as the gunfighter trying to give up the trade but forced to strap on his gun to kill hired gunman Jack Palance. His last film was "The Carpetbaggers" in 1964 (see photo). He died the same year from an overdose of sedatives and alcohol at age 50. (AP Photo via EMPICS)

Burt Lancaster

A circus acrobat before he went into films, Burt Lancaster (shown in "Bird Man Of Alcatraz") could mix all-action with grace, teeth-baring cheerfulness with sometimes frightening inner drives. He was as much at home as a swashbuckler in "The Crimson Pirate" as he was as a vicious gossip columnist in "Sweet Smell Of Success," or the steely-eyed avenger Wyatt Earp in "Gunfight At The OK Corral," or adulterous officer in "From Here To Eternity", or razzamatazz conman evangelist in "Elmer Gantry" (which won him the Best Actor Oscar in 1960). One of the true greats of cinema, Lancaster died in 1994 aged 80.

Jessica Lange

In 1982, versatile Jessica Lange won her first Oscar (for Best Supporting Actress) in "Tootsie" and then the Best Actress Oscar for her performance in "Blue Sky" in 1994. She has built an enviable list of credits in some other excellent movies over the last thirty years, including "The Postman Always Rings Twice," "Cape Fear," and "Sweet Dreams," the biographical film of the life of country singer Patsy Cline.

Charles Laughton

Born in 1899 in England, Charles Laughton was a wonderful character actor proven in a wide range of roles, including King Henry VIII in "The Private Life Of Henry VIII" (for which he won an Oscar for Best Actor in 1933), Captain Bligh in "Mutiny On The Bounty," Quasimodo in "The Hunchback Of Nôtre Dame," and the wily defense attorney in "Witness For The Prosecution." In 1955 he showed what a great director he was with the terrifying "Night Of The Hunter," starring Robert Mitchum. He acted in his last film, "Advise And Consent," in 1962, and died that same year. (AP Photo via EMPICS)

Laurel & Hardy

In over a decade from their first film together in 1927, Stan Laurel and Oliver Hardy (shown in 1945) established themselves as the greatest comedy team in cinema history. Many critics acclaim the 1927 silent "The Battle Of The Century" to be the best comic film ever made, and they were the only silent comedians who were really able to make the transition to sound without difficulty, their verbal humor being just as enjoyable as their visual gags. "The Music Box" won them an Oscar for the Best Short, Comedy, in 1932. They also made feature-length films, but these were not as good and, although they soldiered on until their last, "Atoll K," in 1951, it was a flop. English-born Laurel (real name Arthur Stanley Jefferson) died in 1965; American Norvell Hardy (later known as Oliver) had died in 1957. (AP Photo via EMPICS)

Jude Law

In a little over twelve years English actor Jude Law has appeared in more than twenty-five films, and there are more in the pipeline. Some, to be true, have been flops, while others have shown what a great character actor he has become, none more so than as World War II Russian sniper in "Enemy At The Gates" (2001), and his portrayal of an unflattering hit-man hired to kill Tom Hanks in "Road To Perdition" (2003).

Bruce Lee

American-born Chinese martial arts protagonist Bruce Lee is shown in a scene from the 1973 film, "Enter the Dragon," completed shortly before his death at 32, the cause being ascribed officially as brain edema but which has led to much conjecture. Lee starred in five major movies from 1971 to 1979 (the final two released posthumously), and is credited with influencing and nurturing the understanding of and participation in Chinese martial arts in the West. (AP Photo via EMPICS)

Christopher Lee

Veteran British actor Christopher Lee's greatest creation is Count Dracula, a part he has taken in several films and imbued with such sinister brilliance and malevolence that he is considered the big screen's finest-ever personification of Bram Stoker's vampire. While he has performed in many other horror movies, he has also appeared in a variety of other roles in such films as "The Man With The Golden Gun," "The Lord Of The Rings" and "Star Wars" series, and "Charlie And The Chocolate Factory." Over 80 years of age, he has many projects in the pipeline. (AP Photo via EMPICS)

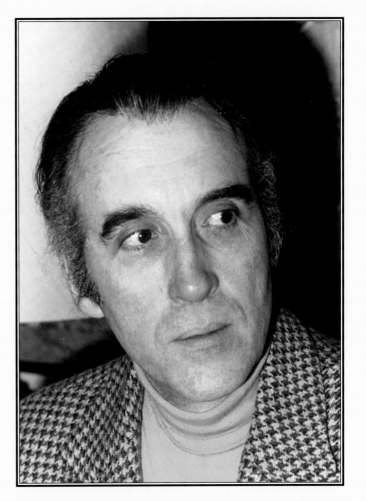

Vivien Leigh

Indian-born to an English father and French/Irish mother, Vivien Leigh was a stage actress who made just eighteen films, winning the Best Actress Oscar for her portrayal of Scarlett O'Hara in "Gone With The Wind" (1939), and another for "A Streetcar Named Desire" (1951) opposite Marlon Brando. Famously married to Laurence Olivier for twenty years, she appeared on stage and screen with him, notably in "The Hamilton Woman" in 1941. Plagued for years with depression, she died of tuberculosis in 1967, aged 53. The photo shows her in character from the 1945 film "Caesar And Cleopatra."

Jack Lemmon

Jack Lemmon was a revered actor whose talents ranged from adroit comedies "The Apartment" and "Some Like It Hot" to the dramatic intensity of "Days of Wine and Roses" and "Tuesdays with Morrie." His screen debut came brilliantly with "It Should Happen To You" (1954) opposite Judy Garland, and he won Oscars for Best Supporting Actor in "Mister Roberts" (1955) and Best Actor for "Save The Tiger" (1972). The photo shows him playing the pivotal role of a power plant engineer devastated by a life-or-death decision he must make in "The China Syndrome" (1979). He died in 2001 at age 76. (AP Photo via EMPICS)

Ray Liotta

Ray Liotta pulls a face at photographers as he arrives at the world premiere of the film "Revolver," in which he appears, in London, September 20, 2005. He has starred in major movies such as "Hannibal" (featuring a shocking scene in which the cannibal Lecter removes the top of the Liotta character's skull and feeds him with part of his own brain) and Martin Scorsese's "GoodFellas," (AP Photo via EMPICS)

Harold Lloyd

Harold Lloyd was the master of the silent-era suspense comedy, mixing laughs with danger by performing humorous stunts in usually perilously lofty places, such as in the 1923 "Safety Last," which features him trying to scale a twenty-story building, hampered by windows, people, mice, and a disintegrating clock face. Enormously popular in the 1920s, he didn't transfer well to the talkies. He is shown, sporting his trademark spectacles, in 1947. (AP Photo via EMPICS)

Sophia Loren

Statuesque, voluptuous Italian beauty Sophia Loren displayed her acting ability when she became the first performer to win the Best Actress Oscar in a foreign-language film, Vittorio de Sica's "Two Women" in 1961. She was probably best suited to big-budget historical epics like "El Cid" and "The Fall Of The Roman Empire," but she was enjoyable to watch in light comedies, too, including "Houseboat" opposite Cary Grant. (AP Photo via EMPICS)

Peter Lorre

One of the screen's greatest villains, Hungarian-born Peter Lorre usually played characters who were easy to despise, hate, and fear, as in the Bogart classics "The Maltese Falcon" and "Casablanca." His whispering voice and toadish looks made him disturbingly menacing. He died in 1964 in his sixtieth year.

Ida Lupino

British actress Ida Lupino made a name for herself as the ideal gangster's moll in the 1940s, often playing the tough but sexy tart, and performing opposite such real screen greats as Humphrey Bogart (in "High Sierra"), Edward G. Robinson (in "The Sea Wolf"), and Richard Widmark (in "Road House"). She is shown in the film "Our Time" in 1944. (AP Photo via EMPICS)

Shirley MacLaine

Shirley MacLaine arrives at the gala for her movie, "In Her Shoes," at the Toronto International Film Festival, September 14, 2005. Nurturing an off-beat, impish persona, she has enjoyed a career of over fifty years, starring in comedies, musicals, and dramas that have included "The Apartment," "Irma La Douce," and "Sweet Charity." The sister of Warren Beatty, she won the Oscar for Best Actress for her performance in "Terms Of Endearment" (1983). (AP Photo via EMPICS)

Steve Martin

Stand-up comedian, actor, writer, musician and composer Steve Martin gestures as he responds to a question at a news conference for his movie "Shopgirl" during the International Film Festival in Toronto, September 9, 2005. He wrote and starred in his first full-length movie, the box office comedy success "The Jerk" in 1979, and has also played in serious roles such as in "Pennies From Heaven" in 1981 and the thriller "The Spanish Prisoner" in 1997. (AP Photo via EMPICS)

Lee Marvin

Lee Marvin is shown giving Jane Fonda some tips on how to handle a six-shooter during a break in filming of the Western movie "Cat Ballou" in 1964, the film that won him an Oscar for Best Actor. Marvin more often played less friendly parts, such as casual, businesslike, ultra-violent criminal, as in "The Big Heat," "The Wild One" (both 1953), and "Point Blank" (1967), and as tough soldier in "The Dirty Dozen," but softened his image in later films such as "The Iceman Cometh" and the political thriller "Gorky Park." He died in 1987 at age 63. (AP Photo via EMPICS)

James Mason

Although he was nominated for an Oscar for "The Verdict" in 1982, it was in the 1940s and '50s that British actor James Mason had his heyday, playing a variety of roles such as fading actor in "A Star Is Born," terrorist in "Odd Man Out," Brutus in "Julius Caesar," professor who falls under a young girl's spell in "Lolita," and mad Captain Nemo in "20,000 Leagues Under The Sea." He died in 1984 aged 79.

The Marx Bros

The Marx Brothers are shown—left to right, Zeppo, Harpo, Chico and Groucho—in 1933. The anarchic (mostly) foursome were regarded as comic geniuses in their heyday in the 1930s, especially in their films "A Night At The Opera" and "A Day At The Races." (AP Photo via EMPICS)

Walter Matthau

The foghorn-voiced film villain of early films in his long career gave way to Walter Matthau becoming a master of crotchety comedy, with his 1966 "The Fortune Cookie" (which first teamed him with Jack Lemmon, and which won him the Oscar for Best Supporting Actor), followed by "The Odd Couple" (which saw him as the slob "husband" battling against his obsessively neat "wife" Lemmon), "Grumpy Old Men" and many other hits. He died at the age of 79 in 2000.

Victor Mature

He may have been more muscle than the big screen's greatest actor, but Victor Mature enjoyed a thirty-year-plus career starring in big-budget epics like "Samson And Delilah" (1949) and "The Robe" (1953), as well as putting in creditable performances as Doc Holliday in John Ford's masterpiece "My Darling Clementine" (1946) and as a trapper in "The Last Frontier" (1956). He died at age 86 in 1999.

Steve McQueen

Exuding a cool, casual insolence with occasional aggressiveness, Steve McQueen was as memorable as a gunfighter in "The Magnificent Seven" and PoW in "The Great Escape" as he was in more cerebral roles like "The Thomas Crown Affair." Projecting a highly sexual image made the girls clamor for him, but the boys, too, were thrilled by his high-speed cop in "Bullitt" and race driver in "Le Mans." One of the top ten box office draws from 1967 to 1976, he died aged 50 in 1980.

Bette Midler

Hawaii-born Bette Midler is a talented actress, comedian, and singer who has had international record hits and has achieved box office screen successes with "The Rose" (as drug-addict rock star Janis Joplin), the drama "Beaches," and "For The Boys" in which she played a 1940s actress/singer.

John Mills

Shown in his uniform as a Second Lieutenant with bride dramatist Mary Hayley Bell in London in 1941, much-revered British actor John Mills had a seventy-year career and won an Oscar for Best Supporting Actor in 1970 for his role as village idiot in "Ryan's Daughter." He was the star in many British films, some of which were international successes, including "Scott Of The Antarctic" in 1948. Father of actresses Juliet and Hayley, he was knighted in 1976. His marriage to Mary lasted sixty-four years until his death at age 97 in 2005; Mary died the same year.

Robert Mitchum

Robert Mitchum, shown in his role in the war epic "Anzio" in 1948, was one of the most important actors to emerge during the 1940s, although he was more popular with audiences than with critics at the time. He established a sleepy-eyed but watchful, laconic persona, hiding toughness and sometimes menace behind a façade of apparent weariness. His fine acting ability was recognized by Charles Laughton who directed him in the frightening *film noir* "The Night Of The Hunter." The *film noir* genre was espoused by Mitchum in his early career, and the film was a cult favorite long after its release. He appeared with, and often out-acted, many top Hollywood stars, including Marilyn Monroe, Deborah Kerr (three times), and Olivia de Havilland, and his portrayal of the disturbed and violent rapist Max Cady in the 1962 version of "Cape Fear" (with Gregory Peck) was one of his very best. (AP Photo via EMPICS)

Marilyn Monroe

Marilyn Monroe poses over the updraft of a New York subway grating while in character for the filming of "The Seven Year Itch" in Manhattan on September 9, 1954. The former Norma Jean Baker starred in twenty-eight movies, many of them box office hits. Sensual and seductive, but with an air of innocence and vulnerability, Monroe became one of the world's most adored sex symbols, her acting talents and screen personality coming to the fore in such movies as "Monkey Business" opposite Cary Grant, her superb performance in "Gentlemen Prefer Blondes" with Jane Russell, and "Some Like It Hot" with Tony Curtis and Jack Lemmon. She died at age 36 in 1962, her death—apparently from an overdose of barbiturates— becoming the subject of many controversial conspiracy theories. (AP Photo via EMPICS)

Demi Moore

As with most movie stars, New Mexico beauty Demi Moore has had highs and lows during her acting career. The highs have included the big-grossing "Ghost" (1990), "A Few Good Men" (1992), and "Indecent Proposal" (1993). But her lows have included her later work, including "The Scarlet Letter" (1995), "The Juror" and "Striptease" (both 1996), and "G.I. Jane" (1997). (AP Photo via EMPICS)

Roger Moore

British actor Roger Moore is shown while on location during filming of the 1973 movie "Live And Let Die," in which he was playing the title role of secret service agent 007, James Bond. Moore starred in seven official Bond movies up to 1985, when he announced his retirement. Having had a successful TV acting career and having appeared in other big screen movies, it is as Bond for which Sir Roger (knighted in 2003) is best known. (AP Photo via EMPICS)

Eddie Murphy

Accomplished comedy actor, stand-up comedian, and singer Eddie Murphy has a penchant for movie series, as in the "Beverly Hills Cop," "Nutty Professor," "Dr. Doolittle" and "Shrek" films, in some of which he plays multiple characters (one way of keeping the money in the family). He has also appeared in one-offs, such as "Trading Places" and "Coming To America."

Liam Neeson

Irish actor Liam Neeson was a strong candidate for the winner of Best Actor Oscar for the 1993 movie "Schindler's List" (which won eight Academy Awards) but had the misfortune of coming up against Tom Hanks' brilliant performance in "Philadelphia." Neeson has since starred in other well-received films, including "Nell," "Rob Roy," "Michael Collins," "Star Wars Episode I: The Phantom Menace," and "Batman Begins."

Paul Newman

For decades, audiences and critics alike have clamored for more Paul Newman movies since his superbly entertaining "The Hustler," "Cool Hand Luke," "The Sting," "The Towering Inferno," "Butch Cassidy And The Sundance Kid," and "The Color Of Money," for which he won the Oscar for Best Actor. He was brilliant again in "Road To Perdition," which he made as he was pushing toward eighty! The photo shows Newman enjoying his off-screen passion as he waits in the driver's seat of his Nissan 300ZX Turbo before the start of a qualifying race at Riverside International Raceway in Los Angeles, October 6, 1984. (AP Photo via EMPICS)

Jack Nicholson

Legendary actor Jack Nicholson is shown posing at a photocall for his movie "Something's Gotta Give" in 2004. He has made audiences cry in sympathy for his Best Actor Oscar-winning performance of a "sane man in a madhouse" in "One Flew Over The Cuckoo's Nest," cry again in fear of his terrifying character in "The Shining," and again with laughter at his obsessive-compulsive in "As Good As It Gets." Throw in "Terms Of Endearment," "The Witches Of Eastwick," "Batman," and "A Few Good Men" and you know you are watching a truly versatile icon of movies.

Nick Nolte

Actor Nick Nolte is shown in a booking photo released September 12, 2002, by the California Highway Patrol, taken after his arrest on suspicion of driving under the influence in Malibu, California. What a shame for a popular actor who has appeared in about fifty films since 1972, including the disturbing thriller "Cape Fear" in 1991 and the heart-wrenching drama "Lorenzo's Oil" in 1992. (AP Photo via EMPICS)

Laurence Olivier

Renowned British stage actor and movie star Laurence Olivier shows Marilyn Monroe the English way to make a movie in 1956, as her director and co-star in "The Prince and the Showgirl." As winner of an Oscar for Best Actor (for "Hamlet" in 1948) Sir Laurence was certainly qualified to teach her. His best films were released between 1939 and 1960, including "Wuthering Heights," "Rebecca," "Henry V," "Richard III," and "The Entertainer," although he did perform chillingly as a former Nazi dentist torturing Dustin Hoffman in "Marathon Man" in 1976. (AP Photo via EMPICS)

Peter O'Toole

While some of Irish actor Peter O'Toole's interesting films have been commercial flops (such as "Lord Jim" and "Great Catherine"), he has certainly made enough box office hits with "Lawrence Of Arabia," "Becket," "What's New Pussycat?" and "The Lion In Winter" to keep him in demand, and in 2003 he received an Honorary Academy Award for his contribution to films. (AP Photo via EMPICS) ◀◀◀

Al Pacino

It's ironic that Al Pacino's hippy but honest cop in "Serpico" (1973) should be straddled by his performances as Mafia member in "The Godfather" (1972) and "The Godfather Part II" (1974). But Pacino carried off both roles well, as throughout his career, and was awarded the Oscar for Best Actor for the 1992 movie "Scent Of A Woman," in which he played a bad-tempered, blind former military officer. Ever willing to stretch himself and take a risk, Pacino plays Shylock the Jew in "The Merchant Of Venice," the 2004 adaptation of William Shakespeare's play. ▶▶▶

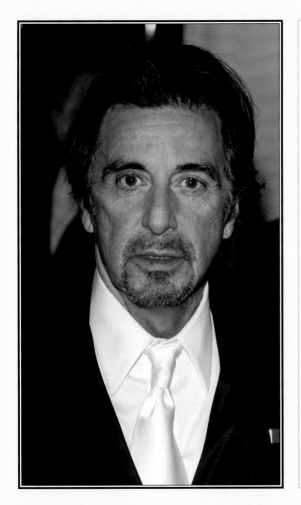

Gwyneth Paltrow

Gwyneth Paltrow made her film debut in "Shout" in 1991, followed quickly by her appearance in "Hook" the same year, and there has hardly been a year ever since that has not seen one of her movies. Many of her performances have achieved critical acclaim, especially "Emma" in 1996, "Shakespeare In Love" in 1998, for which she won an Oscar for Best Actress, "The Royal Tenenbaums" in 2001, and "Proof" in 2005.

Gregory Peck

Usually playing parts involving conflicts in social values, Gregory Peck had an extraordinary record of outstanding performances in major films. In "Twelve O'Clock High" (1949) he had to send his men to possible death on an air mission; in "The Gunfighter" (1950) he was forced to kill to survive; in "MacArthur" he had to disobey his president because of his beliefs; in "The Omen" (1976) he was forced to try to kill his own evil son. He won the Oscar for Best Actor as a small-town lawyer in the 1962 "To Kill A Mockingbird" (see photo). He died at the age of 87 in 2003. (AP Photo via EMPICS)

Sean Penn

Sean Penn has starred in more than forty films, his movie debut coming in the comic "Fast Times At Ridgemont High" in 1982. He received the Academy Award for Best Actor for the 2003 drama "Mystic River." In 2006 fans were eagerly awaiting his next film, "All The King's Men," in which Penn co-stars with Jude Law, Kate Winslet, and Anthony Hopkins. Penn has also directed three films, two of them starring Jack Nicholson ("The Crossing Guard" and "The Pledge"), the other ("The Indian Runner") based on the song "Highway Patrolman" by Bruce Springsteen.

Joe Pesci

At about 5ft 4in, Joe Pesci may not be tall in stature but he's big in talent, especially when he plays a violent mobster as in "Once Upon A Time In America" and "GoodFellas," with buddy Robert de Niro, in whose film "Raging Bull" Pesci made his movie breakthrough. Sometimes his toughie performances have been played for laughs, as in "Home Alone" and "My Cousin Vinny." (AP Photo via EMPICS)

Michelle Pfeiffer

Michelle Pfeiffer has appeared in comedies, such as "Married To The Mob," and thriller/dramas. Her first starring role was in the musical "Grease 2" in 1982, and she sang in "The Fabulous Baker Boys" with real-life brothers Jeff and Beau Bridges. She played a haunted housewife in "What Lies Beneath" with Harrison Ford, co-starred with Glenn Close and John Malkovich in the costume drama "Dangerous Liaisons," and was a pioneering teacher at a tough inner-city school in "Dangerous Minds."

Brad Pitt

One of the sexiest stars in movie history, Brad Pitt got his breakthrough from TV into films with the 1991 road movie "Thelma & Louise," and has hardly looked back since. He competed against the visual impact of Robert Redford's direction of the languid "A River Runs Through It," starred with Morgan Freeman as two cops bringing a serial killer to justice in "Seven," with Bruce Willis in the time-travel sci-fi thriller "12 Monkeys," with Edward Norton in the violent drama "Fight Club," and with Angelina Jolie in the lighter "Mr. & Mrs. Smith."

Sidney Poitier

The first black American to be come a major movie star, Sidney Poitier performed well in "The Defiant Ones" shackled to fellow escaped convict Tony Curtis, and brilliantly as Northern detective opposite bigoted Southern police chief played by Rod Steiger in "In The Heat Of The Night," and was awarded Best Actor Oscar for his 1963 "Lilies Of The Field." He has also directed some of the films he has starred in, as well as others. He is shown accepting the "Distinguished Career" award at the 2005 Film Life Black Movie Awards, October 9, 2005. (AP Photo via EMPICS)

Tyrone Power

A top box office star during the 1940s and '50s, Tyrone Power could perform in a wide range of roles, from musicals to Westerns, from historical epics to courtroom dramas. He was in his forte as swordsman in "The Mark Of Zorro," but ironically died of a heart attack while dueling with George Sanders on the set of "Solomon And Sheba" in 1958. He is shown zipping up Kim Novak's dress in a scene from the 1956 film "The Eddy Duchin Story." (AP Photo via EMPICS)

Vincent Price

Although he'd been acting in movies since 1938, Vincent Price found his niche in the 1950s as a silky-tongued villain in many successful horror films, notably "House Of Wax" and "The Mystery Of The Wax Museum," although his movie career declined as the mocking humor of his style of horror itself went out of fashion for a while. He died in 1993 at the age of 82.

George Raft

Professional boxer-turned-actor George Raft was one of the big four movie gangsters (along with Cagney, Bogart, and Robinson) of the 1930s and '40s. Somewhat wooden, and with an almost expressionless face, Raft nevertheless created a memorable screen presence, exuding sleek menace that was fixed forever in Howard Hawks' 1932 "Scarface."

Robert Redford

Robert Redford was the No. 1 box office star in the 1970s, with blockbuster movies "Butch Cassidy And The Sundance Kid," "All The President's Men," "The Sting," "The Great Gatsby," and "The Way We Were," but his star was prevented from waning by his performances in "Indecent Proposal" in 1993 and "The Horse Whisperer" in 1998. He is also an accomplished director, as shown in his 1980 Oscar-winning "Ordinary People" and in "A River Runs Through It" and "The Horse Whisperer." (AP Photo via EMPICS)

Vanessa Redgrave

Controversial political activist Vanessa Redgrave, a member of the British acting dynasty headed by her late father Michael, won Best Actress Oscar for her performance in the 1977 "Julia," in which she plays a woman fighting fascism in 1930s Europe. Her forthright attack on the extremist Jewish Defense League in her acceptance speech brought both applause and boos. Her other films of note have included "Isadora," "Morgan," and "Mary, Queen Of Scots."

Christopher Reeve

Christopher Reeve was the star in four "Superman" films between 1978 and 1987, was an acclaimed stage actor, and appeared in other films including "The Aviator" (1985) and "Village Of The Damned" (1995). The world was shocked when a horse-riding accident left him quadriplegic in 1995, and saddened at his death in 2004 at the age of 52.

Keanu Reeves

Beirut-born (of an American father and English mother) Keanu Reeves is best known for his starring role in the 1999 sci-fi thriller "The Matrix" and its sequels, although he had already made his name in big-budget movies like "My Own Private Idaho" (1991), the all-action "Speed" (1994), "Johnny Mnemonic" and "Chain Reaction" (both 1995), and has gone on to impress in the 2005 horror "Constantine." (AP Photo via EMPICS)

Tim Robbins

Tim Robbins won the Oscar for Best Supporting Actor for his role in the 2003 "Mystic River." He had already achieved critical acclaim for his performances in the 1992 "The Player" and especially in "The Shawshank Redemption" in 1994. His work as screenwriter, director, and producer has also been recognized, particularly for the death-row movie "Dead Man Walking" (1995) starring his long-term companion Susan Sarandon.

Julia Roberts

By the time she won Best Actress Oscar for her fine performance as true-life anti-corporation pioneer Erin Brockovich in the 2000 movie of the same name, Julia Roberts was already a massive box office star for her romantic comedies "Pretty Woman" (1990) and "Runaway Bride" (1999), both opposite Richard Gere, and the heist movie "Ocean's Eleven."

Edward G. Robinson

Hollywood "gangster" Edward G. Robinson is shown, left, with Gene Kelly, center, and then-Senator Harry S. Truman, Democratic vice-presidential candidate, October 16, 1944, just before the senator made a campaign speech. His short stature and somewhat bulbous features precluded Robinson from undertaking romantic leading-man roles, but he showed his acting brilliance beyond the gangster image in such fine movies as Billy Wilder's "Double Indemnity" (1944), Orson Welles' "The Stranger" (1945), Vincente Minnelli's "Two Weeks In Another Town" (1962), and even in a fairly minor part as the greatest poker player of them all in the 1965 "The Cincinnati Kid," with Steve McQueen. He died in 1973 at the age of 79, and was posthumously awarded an Oscar for his whole career, during which he made more than ninety films. (AP Photo via EMPICS)

Ginger Rogers

The best dancing partner Fred Astaire ever had during ten of the finest musicals of all time, Ginger Rogers was one of the most delightful, wise-cracking showgirls of great comedies in the 1930s and '40s. She will always be remembered for such dancing successes as "Top Hat" (1935), but she also starred in more serious movies like "Kitty Foyle" (1940), for which she was awarded Best Actress Oscar, and "The Major And The Minor" (1942), posing as a twelve-year-old romantically involved with Ray Milland, as well as comedies such as "Monkey Business" (1952) with Cary Grant. She died in 1995 at age 83. (AP Photo via EMPICS)

Mickey Rooney

The diminutive Mickey Rooney was No. 1 box office star in 1939-1941 but became a low-billing performer in cheap films in the 1960s. Born Joseph Yule, Jr., in 1920, he won a Juvenile Oscar in 1938 for "bringing to the screen the spirit and personification of youth," owed a lot of his early success to his role as Andy Hardy in a long-running series of films, played opposite Judy Garland in musicals, and performed serious roles such as a gangster in "Baby Face Nelson" and a solder in "The Bold And The Brave." (AP Photo via EMPICS)

Mickey Rourke

Controversial 1980s leading man Mickey Rourke found box office success in the steamy "9½ Weeks" opposite Kim Basinger, was even sexier in "Angel Heart," and was praised by critics for his performance as an alcoholic writer in "Barfly." Promulgating a "wild man" image, the outspoken Rourke criticized himself and many of those around him, and tried his hand as a professional boxer for a while in the 1990s, but returned to movies in several films, including, in 2005, "Sin City" with Bruce Willis.

Jane Russell

While her voluptuous figure pushed Jane Russell to the fore in the 1940s (notably in the Billy the Kid movie "The Outlaw," which was actually banned for two years after its release in 1943 for being too licentious), she had more to offer than big breasts, as she showed in comedies such as "The Paleface" with Bob Hope and "Gentlemen Prefer Blondes" with Marilyn Monroe, and in more serious roles opposite Hollywood leading men Clark Gable ("The Tall Men") and Robert Mitchum ("His Kind Of Woman"). (AP Photo via EMPICS)

Meg Ryan

Meg Ryan has become best known for playing in romantic comedies (as in her breakthrough movie "When Harry Met Sally...." with Billy Crystal), but has performed in serious roles such as an alcoholic in "When A Man Loves A Woman" and as a military officer in "Courage Under Fire." However, it seems she damaged her screen career when she had an affair in 2001 with Russell Crowe while they were filming "Proof of Life" and while she was still married to Dennis Quaid.

Susan Sarandon

While she appeared in the cult favorite "The Rocky Horror Picture Show" and opposite Robert Redford in "The Great Waldo Pepper" (both 1975), it wasn't until 1988 that she made her breakthrough as a major movie star in the baseball romance "Bull Durham" with Kevin Costner and Tim Robbins (now her long-time companion). She has since gone on to appear in a variety of films, mainly comedies and dramas, and to win a Best Actress Oscar for the 1995 anti-death-penalty "Dead Man Walking," which was directed, co-written and co-produced by Robbins.

Arnold Schwarzenegger

Arnold Schwarzenegger has had a wide and varied career as bodybuilder, massive box office movie star, and high-ranking politician (as governor of California). His most successful films have included "Conan The Barbarian," the all-action "Terminator" series, "Predator," and the comedies "Twins," with Danny DeVito, and "Kindergarten Cop."

George C. Scott

George C. Scott won the Academy Award for Best Actor for the 1969 movie "Patton" (see photo), then famously refused it. By then his acting skills had been displayed in some powerful performances such as prosecuting attorney in "Anatomy Of A Murder" and as hard-man promoter in "The Hustler" (with Paul Newman). He died in 1999, a month short of his 72nd birthday. (AP Photo via EMPICS)

Randolph Scott

Randolph Scott, left, and Cary Grant are shown at the Armstrong-Garcia boxing match in Los Angeles, March 1, 1940. Scott appeared almost exclusively in Westerns from 1946 to 1962, although he had earlier acted in comedies, musicals, and contemporary dramas. For twelve years, he and Grant lived together in a California beach house they named "Bachelor Hall," leading to Hollywood rumors of a homosexual relationship between them. Scott died in 1987 at age 89. (AP Photo via EMPICS)

Peter Sellers

The photo shows English comic actor Peter Sellers in London in 1969. Having already been a hit in the British cinema, Sellers became internationally famous for his portrayal of the bumbling, accident-prone French policeman, Inspector Clouseau, in the "Pink Panther" series of films from 1963, as mad scientist in "Dr. Strangelove or: How I Stopped Worrying And Love The Bomb," Indian doctor (treating Sophia Loren) in "The Millionairess," and nutty psychiatrist in "What's New Pussycat?" He died in 1980 aged 54.

Omar Sharif

Egyptian actor Omar Sharif rode a camel into international stardom in the 1962 epic "Lawrence Of Arabia," and, among many films in a fifty-year career up to 2003, has been cast as exotic lover with flashing eyes, such as in the hugely successful "Doctor Zhivago" (1965) and "The Tamarind Seed" (1974), as well as heroic captain of a ship with a bomb on board in "Juggernaut" (1974), and as a gambler in "Funny Girl" (1968). (AP Photo via EMPICS)

William Shatner

Canadian-born William Shatner, left, poses with DeForest Kelley, center, and Leonard Nimoy on the set of the television series "Star Trek." Shatner played Captain Kirk in six "Star Trek" movies between 1979 and 1991, directing one of them. Rumors of his character's and his resurrection in a further "Star Trek" movie have proven to be unfounded. (AP Photo via EMPICS)

Frank Sinatra

The photo shows Frank Sinatra in the brilliant musical "On The Town" in 1950. His other great musicals included ""Guys And Dolls" and "High Society." One of the most popular singers of the last century, Sinatra could easily have made it big in movies even without a singing and dancing career, such was his acclaimed talent as an actor in such classics as "From Here To Eternity" (1953) that won him a Best Supporting Actor Oscar, "The Man With The Golden Arm" (1955), "The Manchurian Candidate" (1962), and "Von Ryan's Express" in 1965. (AP Photo via EMPICS)

Maggie Smith

British stage and screen actress Maggie Smith is shown at the premiere of her latest Harry Potter film, "Harry Potter And The Goblet Of Fire," November 6, 2005. In a movie career lasting over forty years her prodigious acting talent has been displayed in "The Pride Of Miss Jean Brodie" (1968), which won her the Academy Award for Best Actress, and "California Suite" (1977) for which she received the Oscar for Best Supporting Actress. (AP Photo via EMPICS)

Will Smith

Movie actor, TV star, and recording artist Will Smith has appeared in several box office hits, including "Independence Day" (1996), "Men In Black" (1997), "Enemy Of The State" (1998), "Ali" (2001), and "I, Robot" (2004).

Kevin Spacey

Stage and screen actor Kevin Spacey won the Best Actor Oscar for his part as a lustful suburban father in "American Beauty" (1999) following his Best Supporting Actor Academy Award for his criminal in "The Usual Suspects" (1995). He has also starred as a serial killer in "Seven" (also 2005), as a troubled journalist in "The Shipping News" (2001), and as singer Bobby Darin in "Beyond The Sea" (2004), which he also directed and co-wrote, and in which he sings Darin's top hits. (AP Photo via EMPICS)

Sylvester Stallone

Sylvester Stallone poses in character as "Rocky," the fictional boxer he portrayed in a series of blockbuster films starting in 1976. Stallone wrote the screenplay for the first film, which won the Oscar for Best Film, and also won the Oscar for Best Director. He also starred as John Rambo in "First Blood (1982) and in the Rambo sequels. (AP Photo via EMPICS)

Barbara Stanwyck

Barbara Stanwyck developed a successful screen persona as a tender and vulnerable woman on the inside, yet gutsy, independent and at times ruthless on the surface, playing a stripper on the make in "Ball Of Fire" (1941) and a double-crossing wife luring Fred MacMurray to murder in "Double Indemnity" (1944). Her range also included comic and sexy roles. Here, she is shown in the title role with her daughter, played by Anne Shirley, in the 1937 film, "Stella Dallas." She died in 1990 in her 83rd year, having made almost 100 movies, receiving an Honorary Academy Award in 1982 for her career's work. (AP Photo via EMPICS)

Rod Steiger

Rod Steiger was a superb Method-style actor who could play theatrical and mannered roles, once adopting seven disguises for his starring role in "No Way To Treat A Lady" (1968). His looks and size steered him more to heavies rather than to romantic leads, so we saw him in "On The Waterfront" in 1954, and as "Al Capone" in 1959, and a stubborn small-town police chief in "In The Heat Of The Night" (1967). He died in 2002 at the age of 77. (AP Photo via EMPICS)

James Stewart

Although he played in some great Westerns, James Stewart was just as effective in non-Western parts and is considered one of the very best movie stars of all time, earning an Oscar for Best Actor as a young reporter in "The Philadelphia Story" in 1941, and an Honorary Academy Award for Lifetime Achievement in 1985. His incredibly flexible range included an honest idealist fighting corruption in "Mr. Smith Goes to Washington" (1939) and cold, hard bounty hunter in "The Naked Spur" (1953), a good-natured drunk in "Harvey" (1950) and suicidal family man in the classic "It's A Wonderful Life" (1946). He died in 1997 at age 89. (AP Photo via EMPICS)

Sharon Stone

Although she appeared in inconsequential movies in the 1980s, Sharon Stone's part in the Arnold Schwarzenegger film "Total Recall" boosted her career, helped by her nude pose in "Playboy" magazine that coincided with the film's release in 1990. Considered one of the sexiest women in the world, she really hit the box office charts as a drug-taking serial killer in the erotic "Basic Instinct" opposite Michael Douglas in 1992, and her role in Martin Scorsese's "Casino" in 1995 achieved critical acclaim. Fans eagerly await "Basic Instinct 2: Risk Addiction."

Meryl Streep

Testament to Meryl Streep's fine movie acting ability is the fact that she has been nominated for thirteen Academy Awards (more than any other performer), winning as Best Supporting Actress for "Kramer vs Kramer" in 1980 and as Best Actress for "Sophie's Choice" in 1983. Other films of particular note have included "The French Lieutenant's Woman" (1981), "Out Of Africa" (1985), and her excellent performance in "The Bridges Of Madison County" (1995).

Barbra Streisand

One of the most successful singers ever, Barbra Streisand is also an accomplished movie actress, director, and producer. In 1968 she shared (with Katherine Hepburn) the Academy Award for Best Actress for her first film, "Funny Girl," and went on to win another Oscar as Composer for the song "Evergreen" from her 1976 film "A Star Is Born." Her acting range is such that she has starred in both screwball comedies and dramas.

Donald Sutherland

Canadian-born Donald Sutherland made his best films in the 1960s and '70s, including "The Dirty Dozen," as Captain "Hawkeye" Pierce in "M*A*S*H," "Kelly's Heroes," and "The Eagle Has Landed." More recently, he has performed notably in non-war films, and particularly as scene-stealer father of daughters in the critically acclaimed "Pride And Prejudice" (2005).

Elizabeth Taylor

British-born Elizabeth Taylor is shown with fellow English actor Laurence Harvey in a scene from the 1960 movie "Butterfield 8," for which Taylor won her first Best Actress Academy Award; her second was for the 1966 "Who's Afraid Of Virginia Woolf?" which is reckoned to be her finest performance. The Hollywood icon, twice-married to and divorced from the late Richard Burton (and married six other times), built a reputation as an actress and star in a wide variety of roles, including, as a child, in "National Velvet" with Mickey Rooney, "Father Of The Bride" with Spencer Tracy, "Giant" with James Dean, "Raintree County" with Montgomery Clift, and "Cat On A Hot Tin Roof" with Paul Newman. In more recent years she has been plagued with injuries and ill-health. (AP Photo via EMPICS)

Spencer Tracy

Many of Spencer Tracy's best films were made with long-time companion Katherine Hepburn (they are shown together in a scene from the 1938 film "Adam's Rib"). Regarded by some as one of the greatest Hollywood actors of all, Tracy won the Best Actor Academy Award two years in a row, for the 1937 "Captains Courageous" and the 1938 "Boy's Town." Tracy was thirty-seven years in the movies, completing his last film, "Guess Who's Coming To Dinner" with Hepburn, just seventeen days before he died in 1967 at the age of 67. (AP Photo via EMPICS)

John Travolta

While not becoming typecast, John Travolta shot to stardom in the late 1970s in two sensational teen music/dance films, "Saturday Night Fever" (see photo) and "Grease." He has also starred in Quentin Tarantino's cult movie "Pulp Fiction" (1994), "Get Shorty" (1995), "Face/Off" (1997), "The General's Daughter" (1999), and as former President Bill Clinton in "Primary Colors" (1998). (AP Photo via EMPICS)

Lana Turner

Sexy "Sweater Girl" of World War II, Lana Turner may not have been a brilliant actress, but she certainly had screen dominance. (Kirk Douglas, following their appearance in the 1953 movie "The Bad And The Beautiful," is reported to have told her, "You acted badly and you moved clumsily, but the point is every eye in the audience was on you.") Another of her notable performances was as a broad persuading John Garfield to murder her husband in the 1946 "The Postman Always Rings Twice." She died in 1995 at age 74. (AP Photo via EMPICS)

Rudolph Valentino

A star for only six years in the 1920s, Italian-born Rudolph Valentino was a massive box office draw during the silent era, especially for women, who drooled over his smoldering sex appeal and his reputation as the great lover. His 1921 movie "The Four Horsemen Of The Apocalypse" was one of the biggest commercial successes of all time, launching the romantic Latin lover with the flashing eyes, flaring nostrils, and sleek black hair into legend. He died from peritonitis in 1926 at the age of 31.

Denzel Washington

Much-respected actor Denzel Washington's big break into stardom came when he played South African anti-apartheid campaigner Steve Biko in Richard Attenborough's 1987 film "Cry Freedom," and he went on to win an Oscar for Best Supporting Actor as a slave in the 1989 movie "Glory." Continuing to play parts in movies with "meaning," he starred in "Malcolm X" in 1992, and won the Oscar for Best Actor as a corrupt police officer in the 2001 "Training Day."

John Wayne

Without doubt the No. 1 Western star, John Wayne is considered by many to be the greatest movie star of all time, rating a top ten place almost every year from 1949 to 1974. Some critics claim he was more a "natural" performer than good actor, but he was a consummate master of timing, using his abilities to extraordinary effect, from the shy, almost diffident Ringo Kid in one of his earliest films, the 1939 "Stagecoach," to the resigned and dying gunfighter in his final movie, the 1976 "The Shootist." In between he had played in blockbuster World War II films, dusty cavalry epics, as Davy Crocket in "The Alamo," the sheriff in arguably the best Western of all, "Rio Bravo," the retired boxer in possibly his best film, "The Quiet Man," and as the memorable one-eyed, cantankerous gunfighter in the 1969 "True Grit," for which he was awarded a belated Oscar for Best Actor. He died in 1979 at age 72. (AP Photo via EMPICS)

Sigourney Weaver

Tall, willowy beauty Sigourney Weaver is best known for her performances as Lieutenant Ellen Ripley in Ridley Scott's 1979 movie "Alien" (see photo) and its sequels, and for her Dana Barrett in the 1984 "Ghostbusters" and "Ghostbusters II" in 1989, although she was brilliant in the part of the bitchy Katherine Parker in "Working Girl," with Harrison Ford and Melanie Griffith. (AP Photo via EMPICS)

Johnny Weissmuller

A mermaid was the last thing Tarzan (Johnny Weissmuller) was fishing for, but his catch resulted in an exciting adventure in "Tarzan And The Mermaids," in 1948. Fifteen actors played Tarzan on screen, the Austro-Hungarian-born Olympic Gold Medalist and world record swimmer Weissmuller being the most popular, playing the part in twelve movies. He played thirteen times as "Jungle Jim" in another series, although other films he made were not as well received. He died in 1984 in his 79th year. (AP Photo via EMPICS)

Orson Welles

The photo shows Orson Welles as black marketeer Harry Lime in the 1949 film, "The Third Man." Welles was one of the most important directors in the history of cinema, his movies "Citizen Kane" (1941) and "Touch Of Evil" (1958)—in both of which he also starred—being hailed as being among the best films ever made. He was also a most influential screenwriter and producer. He died in 1985 at the age of 70. (AP Photo via EMPICS)

155

Mae West

Full-bodied Mae West was one of the great screen comediennes, as well as being a brilliant writer for stage and screen, her delightfully bawdy lines being oft-quoted (such as her "Why don't you come up some time, see me"—slightly altered in popular usage—to Salvation Army man Cary Grant in "She Done Him Wrong" in 1933). Many of her films were censored, but she found ways to slip *double entendres* past the censors. Her heyday was a period in the 1930s and '40s, although she did appear in movies as late as 1978. She died at the age of 87 in 1980. (AP Photo via EMPICS)

Richard Widmark

Richard Widmark's movie career started as the giggling, hysterically laughing, psychotic killer pushing a little old lady down a flight of stairs in the 1947 "Kiss Of Death." It may have been his finest film, but he has performed outstandingly in many other roles, often incorporating nasty traits into the behavior of his heroes. He was a vicious cop in "Madigan" (1968) and a drunken Jim Bowie in "The Alamo" (1960), as well as being charismatic in thrillers such as "The Street With No Name" (1948), war films and psychological dramas.

Robin Williams

Many of Robin Williams' movies have been comedies (such as "Mrs Doubtfire" in 1993), and he has displayed a penchant for performing a wide variety of characters in serious roles, such as the inspirational teacher in "Dead Poets Society" in 1989), a pediatrician in the drama "What Dreams May Come" (1998), and as a psychologist in "Good Will Hunting" in 1997, for which he received the Academy Award for Best Supporting Actor.

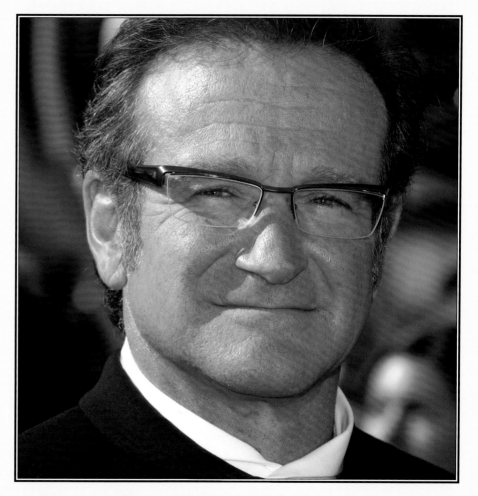

Bruce Willis

Born in Germany to an American father and German mother, Bruce Willis is best known for his all-action "Die Hard" series of films released from 1988 to 1995, although he has appeared in a variety of other roles such as in "The Bonfire Of The Vanities" (1990), "Pulp Fiction" in 1994, "12 Monkeys" in 1995, and "The Whole Nine Yards" (which he also produced) in 2000.

Kate Winslet

English actress Kate Winslet had her first starring role in "Heavenly Creatures" in 1994 but it was for her role in the blockbuster "Titanic" in 1997 that she became a massive movie star. She has been nominated for Academy Awards four times, the most recent for her performance in the romantic film "Eternal Sunshine Of The Spotless Mind" in 2004.

Shelley Winters

As much at home playing a tough and pretty floozy or a tough and blowsy mother, Shelley Winters won Best Supporting Oscars for "The Diary Of Anne Frank" in 1959 and for "A Patch Of Blue" in 1965. Many of her characters died (for example, the new wife killed by Robert Mitchum in "Night Of The Hunter," James Mason's wife run over by an automobile in "Lolita," and the heroine swimmer who rescued Gene Hackman in "The Poseidon Adventure" only to die of exhaustion). Winters herself died in 2006 in her 86th year. (AP Photo via EMPICS)

Renée Zellweger

Renée Zellweger has displayed prodigious box office attraction and no little talent in more than twenty-five films since 1993, breaking through with her starring role opposite Tom Cruise in "Jerry Maguire" in 1996, piling on the pounds for her two "Bridget Jones" films (2001 and 2004), showing fleetness of foot in the excellent musical "Chicago" with Catherine Zeta-Jones in 2002, and winning the Best Supporting Actress Oscar for the 2003 "Cold Mountain."

Catherine Zeta-Jones

Welsh beauty Catherine Zeta-Jones (married to Michael Douglas) earned fame in starring roles opposite Antonio Banderas in "The Mask Of Zorro" (1998) and Sean Connery in "Entrapment" 1999. She was excellent in the 2002 musical "Chicago," for which she won the Best Supporting Actress Oscar, was wily opposite George Clooney in "Intolerable Cruelty" (2003), and was swashbuckling again in "The Legend of Zorro" in 2005. (AP Photo via EMPICS)